MAJOR DECISIONS

The Guide to College Majors

Fifth Edition

Richard A. Blumenthal, M.S.

Joseph A. Despres, Ed. D.

ISBN: 9798503307092

BISAC: STU010000, STU009000, EDU002000

majordecisionsbook@gmail.com

Acknowledgements

For Linda and our children, Sarah and Emily. - *R.A.B.*

This book is dedicated to my wife, Kathleen, for her patience and encouragement through the many hours of preparing the manuscript, and my sons, Michael and David. - *J.A.D.*

About the Authors

Richard A. Blumenthal, M.S. is a Licensed School Counselor, a Nationally Certified Counselor (retired), and a Licensed Mental Health Counselor (retired). He is the author of numerous professional works published in such peer reviewed journals as *The Journal of Human Behavior and Learning*, *Medical Hypnoanalysis*, *The International Journal of Psychosomatics*, *The British Journal of Clinical and Experimental Hypnosis*, and many others. He is the originator of the Rational Suggestion Therapy (RST) counseling technique, and is the inventor of a computer hypnosis method, for which he was awarded a United States Patent. Mr. Blumenthal is also the author of the award-winning novel, *The Freedom Game.*

Dr. Joseph A. Despres, Ed. D. was a middle school and high school counselor for many years. He holds a Doctor of Education degree from Teachers College, Columbia University, and is currently an Assistant Professor, Department of Counseling and Development, Long Island University. He is a former associate editor of the *Journal of World Education* and belongs to many counseling professional associations.

Table of Contents

Read Me. Really.

Every college has one thing they all agree on.

There are literally thousands of colleges in the USA. They're large, small, in the heart of a city, or out in the wide open spaces. They all have one thing in common. They insist that their students choose and fulfill the requirements of a major. If you think that means a college major is pretty important, you're right. We think it's the most important part of your college search!

Do we know what they're talking about?

Add us up and we have over a half century of real life experience as school counselors. We have helped thousands of students search for, and gain admission to hundreds of colleges. We've taught other counselors how to help their students. We wrote the original, much-copied version of this book, now updated for the 21st century. We're on your side. Our only goal is to help you find the right school for you. We're sure this book can be an important part of your search.

It's really such a *major* decision?

You bet it is. First of all, the cost of a four-year college education is kind of like buying a house. Between the tuition, room and board, books, transportation, and other necessaries, the money alone gives you every reason to choose wisely. But there's more. It's four years of your life! It also leads to your future career! That's quite an investment. You might say, major. This calls for some real thought and research. You could just throw a dart at the map and shout, "I'll go here!" Not what we recommend. Hence, the college search is the way to go.

Search as a consumer, not a beggar.

Many students approach their college search as beggars. "Please, somebody, anybody, accept me." This is very wrong. Without you and other students like you, most of the thousands of colleges in the USA wouldn't exist. They need you. They need the money you bring in, and they need for you to succeed. Your attendance and success is what makes them a legitimate institution, a going concern. College is a big business. More importantly to you, college is largely a consumer-based industry, and you, the student, are the consumer. Those would be very empty buildings and lonely professors without students. Colleges can, and do, go out of business, and they know it. So, for the moment, let's stop thinking like beggars and more like shoppers. The idea is to end up with something that's worth all the time and money you're investing.

What is a college search, anyway?

Let's stick with the shopping idea. Not for groceries, but for a very big ticket item, like a house where the decision will change the course of your life. To make a good purchase, you must first know what you want to buy. In the case of a house, it might be a question of how many bedrooms, how many bathrooms, etc. In the case of a college, the factors might include location, size, sports, and other things. However, by far, the most important factor in your college search is the majors offered. If they aren't selling what you want to buy, then why?

What is a college major?

Put simply, it is the one subject area where you will take the most courses in order to develop an expertise in the field. To earn your degree, colleges insist that you choose and declare the major of your choice. Then they expect you to fulfill the course requirements they have set out for the major you've chosen. Usually, you have until the junior year of college to choose, but, for some majors, they may even want you to tell them on the application, so you can start the preliminary courses for that major right away.

When friends and family find out you're in college, the first thing they'll ask you is, "What's your major?" Of course, there's no one thing that defines you as a person, but as a college student, asking about your major is very much like asking, "What do you do for a living?" The major you choose reaches far beyond college graduation because it will contain the courses and advisement that will lead to a career. You might even say, the college major is the start of your career. Doing well in your major by getting great grades and learning a lot is what an employer or graduate school in your field wants to see after you graduate.

Not every college offers every major.

Here's why it's so important to your college search. To state the obvious, you can only take the courses offered by the college you attend. If there's a major you want to study and it's not offered in the school you chose, you chose the wrong school. Period. You will not get the education you wanted. Even if you get great grades in what you take, if the major is not what you wanted, it's the wrong school. Having some idea of what you might want to study is essential.

When should I start thinking about majors?

That's easy. The earlier the better. Traveling without directions, a map, or a GPS, you can drive and drive, making random turns, and never get where you want to go. You may even run out of power and get stuck on the side of the road in the middle of nowhere. All too often, people are forced to settle for something they didn't want simply because they didn't plan ahead.

Randomness can be fun sometimes, it's true, but gambling casinos know that gamblers randomly rolling the dice lose more than they win. Big, life-sized choices are best made based on information and thoughtful planning. To avoid losing at college casino, please take the relatively small amount of effort needed to give this book a going over. We've tried to make using it as painless as possible by compiling and organizing information from many, many sources for you. One piece of information will lead to another, bounce over to another, and maybe yet another, until you have a pretty good idea of what you might want your future college to offer.

So, when should you start? As you'll see in a minute, one of the sections we included in each major listing is called 'Suggested High School Subjects'. That's because the courses you take in high school are directly preparing you for the courses you will take in college, including the ones in your major. Colleges know this. What you learn in high school doesn't just help you to do well in your college courses. It also helps you get into the colleges that offer what you want. When a college admissions person evaluates your high school transcript, it's not just your grade point average they're looking at. They want to see what courses you took and how well you did in the courses that will matter the most in college. If, in your application essay, you state that you're driven to be a physician, but you barely passed biology, how do you think that will go over? College preparation is something to be taken seriously from the very start of high school.

Okay. Calm down. Take a deep breath. Let it out. Even if you're a high school senior, and you suddenly realize that you didn't take high school seriously enough, there's still hope. Colleges will sometimes ask students to prove themselves with more elementary courses and then allow them to take the more difficult ones associated with the chosen major. Another approach is to begin taking courses at a college with easier admissions, get great grades, and then transfer to the college that offers the major you want to pursue. Early or late, plan when you can.

Here's why you need this book.
Most people can name a few well-known majors off the top of their head. Ten would be a lot. Twenty is remarkable. That's fine, except there are dozens and dozens. There are many majors you've never heard of, yet might find fascinating. 150 are described in this book. Having them all in one place, you'll learn a lot about what's out there. You'll also find that, with a little effort, it's not too hard to narrow things down. Searching is as much about what you don't want, as it is about pinpointing what you do want. Arriving at your short list of majors is a lot easier if you look through the listings and rule them out as you go along. After that, what's left are the ones you examine more closely. We've also provided a section of related majors, so, if you find one major interesting, you can flip to some others that might also be interesting, too. More on that in a minute.

Talking to college admissions counselors is very important.

This is true for a couple of reasons. Yes, you're a consumer, but admission to college is a two way street. You choose to apply. They choose to accept. Many colleges receive far more applications than openings they have for new students. To make a decision about whether to accept you, they mainly want to know that you'll be successful at their school. You can show them in various ways, such as your high school grades, the courses you took, your test scores, interview, activities, etc. Don't let the admissions process get in the way of applying to the schools that have the majors that interest you. When you're afraid to apply, you take yourself out of the game. You're already making the decision for them. You reject yourself before they even have a chance to know you. Making a connection with an admissions counselor at a college that interests you will show your enthusiasm for what you can accomplish there. Make that connection during your search, before you even apply. They'll be looking for your application.

Now, let's get back to the 'search' reason for talking with admissions. Colleges often put their own spin on the titles they give their majors. There may be several perfectly acceptable names for essentially the same major. In some of the listings you'll find in this book, we mention some alternative names, but even if we don't, it's true for just about every one. If, after looking over a college's website, you aren't sure that a particular major they offer is the one you're looking for, it's a great idea to ask an admissions counselor, "I'm interested in _____. Is there a major at your school that will prepare me for a career in that?" Or, "I read about a major in _____. What do you call that major in your school?" Asking questions like these, you've just done some very important things. You told them that you have a plan for your future. You showed them that you're serious about wanting a college to fit your plan, and you're hoping that their college is the best one for you. That's big stuff to a college admissions person. Way bigger than, "What's the meal plan like?" Food is important, of course, but questions about what you can study leaves the impression of a serious student.

How to Use This Book

Let's dissect the various parts. Feel free to mix and match.

Read Me. Really.

If you didn't read it, please read it. Really.

Table of Contents

Lists the majors in alphabetical order, with a page number where each can be found. One way to get started is to skim through the entire list and make a note of titles that sound interesting. Then visit those pages at your leisure.

The Majors

Information about each major listing is organized into the following sections:

Major Title

The name by which the major is commonly called. The same or a very similar major may be called by other names in different colleges.

Description

A definition of the major and some insights about the academic or occupational field it comes from.

Plan of Study

How colleges will likely want a student to proceed in order to complete the major. It may include special requirements of various kinds, such as internships, laboratory research, culminating projects, and more. Also, the plan of study may discuss what must be accomplished in the lower division, in order to move on to the more intense upper division courses.

Expect to Take

This is a list of college course titles many colleges require students to take in this major.

General Interest Areas

If you like these, you would probably enjoy this major.

Suggested High School Subjects

A list of courses to take in high school that would help to prepare you for success in this major.

Some Career Possibilities

A list of some of the careers that could eventually come from studying this major. It is important to note that many of the careers listed may not immediately lead to a listed career, but may require a graduate degree, certification, or other training prior to working in the field. Still, the major would most likely be a good start on the road to a promising career from the list.

Some Related Majors

If you found this one intriguing, this is a list of majors that you might want to look into, also appearing in the book.

Some Useful Terms

Degree

Awarded by a college to certify that the person named has successfully fulfilled the college's requirements and completed the degree program specified. Some types of degrees are listed below.

Undergraduate

Coursework in a two or four year degree program.

Graduate

Coursework beyond the four year degree.

Lower Division

First and second years of a four year degree. Sometimes called Freshman and Sophomore years.

Upper Division

Third and fourth years of a four year degree. Sometimes called Junior and Senior years.

Declaring a Major

Many colleges ask students to identify their likely major on an application, but give a lot of leeway in changing majors during the first two years. Students are usually required to formally declare a major prior to entering the Junior year. However, there are many majors that require special lower division coursework in order to declare the major in the upper division. That's one reason why mapping out a plan of study could be important.

License or Certification

Credentials granted by the State you plan to work in, permitting the holder to practice a particular profession after completing that State's training requirements.

A.A.

Associate of Arts, a two year degree. Not discussed much in this book. Majors in associate degree programs are largely vocational or prepare students to transfer to another college to complete a major for a four year degree.

B.A.

Bachelor of Arts, a four year degree usually involving some liberal arts and/or foreign language. Sometimes referred to as a Baccalaureate degree.

B.S.

Bachelor of Science, a four-year degree. Sometimes referred to as a Baccalaureate degree.

B.M.

Bachelor of Music, a four year degree concentrating in music.

B.F.A.

Bachelor of Fine Arts, a four year degree with a concentration in one of the arts.

B.B.A.

Bachelor of Business Administration, a four year degree concentrating in a business major

M.A.

Master of Arts, a graduate degree usually two or three years beyond the four year degree.

M.S.

Master of Science, a graduate degree usually two or three years beyond the four year degree.

Ph. D.

Doctor of Philosophy, a graduate degree beyond the Master's degree, culminating in a dissertation and granting the graduate the right to use the salutation, Dr. in front of their name.

Ed. D.

Doctor of Education, a graduate degree in education beyond the Master's degree, culminating in a dissertation and granting the graduate the right to use the salutation, Dr. in front of their name

J.D.

Juris Doctor, a graduate degree beyond the four year degree, preparing students to practice law.

M.D.

Medical Doctor, a graduate degree beyond the four year degree, preparing students to be physicians.

O.D.

Doctor of Osteopathy, a medical graduate degree beyond the four year degree preparing students to be physicians.

The Majors

ACCOUNTING

Description
The major in accounting is the professional study of keeping and managing financial statements. It includes the compilation of financial information for use in making economic decisions. More than the keeping of business records found in account books and ledgers, it requires an understanding of those business transactions that have an impact on the business or other organization, whether positive or negative, and the reproduction of these transactions as a part of the financial statement.

Plan of Study
The plan of study usually calls for the completion of courses that will make one eligible to sit for the certified public accountant (C.P.A.) examination. The undergraduate degree can be awarded as a bachelor of science or as a bachelor of business administration. The major also may be combined with subjects such as economics, finance, or general management in a dual major program.

Expect to Take
Principles of accounting, tax accounting, cost accounting, principles of finance, business law, money and banking, calculus and advanced calculus, fundamentals of computer programming.

Suggested High School Subjects
Advanced mathematics, business electives, social studies electives, computer studies. (warning: over-specialization in business courses at the high school level could be viewed as vocational and not college preparation.)

General Interest Areas
Mathematics, business, law, finance.

Some Career Possibilities

accountant (C.P.A.)	banking trainee	bursar
F.B.I. agent	management consultant	tax accountant
auditor	budget accountant	comptroller
Internal Revenue Service agent	small business owner	teacher

Some Related Majors

applied mathematics computer science	economics	business eco.
banking and finance	business administration	marketing
business statistics	insurance	

ADVERTISING

Description
Advertising is a specialty within the area of business. It examines the techniques used to communicate a message, whether in print or through the audio/visual media, attempting to persuade readers, viewers, or listeners to take some kind of action or change their life, such as to buy a product, or support a cause or candidate.

Plan of Study
Undergraduate programs in advertising include courses such as consumer behavior (exploring factors or conditions which lead people to buy), market research (gathering information needed to know sales potential of a product), principles of advertising, and sales management. Core courses in business organization, finance, and accounting will also be included.

Expect to Take
Introduction to psychology, statistics in business, operations research, algebra and calculus in business, advertising.

Suggested High School Subjects
Advanced English with emphasis on writing skills, advanced social studies, business and art electives, computer-aided art and design.

General Interest Areas
Communications, social science, business, art and design.

Some Career Possibilities
business education teacher	public relations specialist	purchasing agent
market research analyst	sales manager	sales rep.
buyer	credit analyst	
fundraiser	manager	

Some Related Majors
business administration	marketing	fashion merch.
journalism	English	radio/television
communications	media study	fine arts

AEROSPACE ENGINEERING

Description
Also titled "Aeronautical Engineering" or "Astronautical Engineering," this is the study of the design, construction, and operation of aircraft. Today, the field has been broadened to mean the design, construction, and operation of all vehicles that operate above the earth's surface. Within this major are incorporated topics including fuselage design, wing design, structural design, structural requirements, propulsion mechanisms, fuel types, guidance and instrumentation systems, auxiliary equipment, and production.

Plan of Study
The plan of study is a demanding one. Core courses include basic engineering theory, physics, and calculus and differential equations, which lead to specialized study of topics including aerodynamics, wind flow, computer programming, and flight simulation. Students also may be expected to conduct their own experiments under the supervision of an instructor.

Expect to Take
Aerodynamics, fluid dynamics, flow noise, advanced flight dynamics, inertial engineering, structural design, computer-aided design, special projects, individual supervised research.

Suggested High School Subjects
Advanced social studies, advanced mathematics through calculus, advanced science through physics with lab, foreign language, computer studies.

General Interest Areas
Mathematics, science, flight, experimentation.

Some Career Possibilities
aerospace engineer	college professor	lawyer
aircraft design engineer	commercial pilot	meteorologist
astronaut	entrepreneur	technical writer
astrophysicist	flight engineer	test pilot

Some Related Majors
applied mathematics	electrical engineering	mechanical eng.
astrophysics	environmental	physics
earth sciences	engineering	

AFRICAN STUDIES

Description
African studies is one of several categories of majors considered as area studies. It concerns the study of the African continent and its people, from the earliest times to the present. This major is often undertaken prior to, or together with, work in law, foreign service, or diplomacy as an undergraduate study; some colleges combine it with anthropology, economics, history, politics, sociology, or other subjects as a dual major program.

Plan of Study
The plan of study includes history of the African peoples, their origin from earliest known times, the development of various peoples into tribes and nations, economic life, and traditional practices. The origins and rise of different cultures, folklore, and religious practices are also studied, as well as the emergence of northern and southern (that is, sub-Saharan) national groups, colonialism, and political movements of the twentieth century.

Expect to Take
Introduction to anthropology, history of Africa, Islam in Africa, politics in Africa, colonialism and modernization, economic growth, the Near East and Africa, northern Africa, Saharan and sub-Saharan Africa.

Suggested High School Subjects
Advanced social studies, foreign language, advanced English, computer literacy

General Interest Areas
History, law, politics, social science, communications, languages

Some Career Possibilities

college professor	freelance writer	political scientist
counselor	lawyer	social worker
diplomat	government area	teacher
education consultant	specialist	
foreign service officer	military officer	

Some Related Majors

American studies	area studies	international rel.
anthropology	comparative literature	political science
archaeology	foreign languages	sociology

AFRO-AMERICAN STUDIES

Description
This major consists of the study of the history and culture of Black Americans, with special emphasis upon the contributions to American society. Sometimes called "Black Studies," this major seeks to provide students with a thorough and accurate understanding of the development of black culture in America. A significant feature of this major is an examination of the economic, social, artistic, and political forces shaping black culture in historic and contemporary American life.

Plan of Study
The plan of study is usually interdisciplinary in nature, and begins as a liberal arts study, with coursework ranging from composition through history, psychology, and social science. At the upper-division level, coursework includes history of Black Americans in various regions of the nation, as well as black art, music, poetry, politics, religion, and literature. Independent research on selected topics of current interest is usually encouraged.

Expect to Take
Introduction to black studies, black history, black music and art, black literature of the nineteenth century, contemporary black literature, political movements among black Americans, independent study.

Suggested High School Subjects
Advanced social studies, mathematics through algebra, science through biology, foreign language, electives in psychology and sociology, computer literacy.

General Interest Areas
Black history, music, literature, research, data collection.

Some Career Possibilities
historian	librarian	freelance writer
anthropologist	clergy/counselor	social worker
lawyer	museum curator	sociologist
journalist	college professor	
book editor	researcher	

Some Related Majors
African studies	area studies	secondary ed.
American studies	art history/appreciation	social psychology
anthropology	history	sociology

AGRICULTURAL BUSINESS AND ECONOMICS

Description
This specialized major studies the relationship of economics and industrial practices in agricultural production. The management of farms, ranches, and farm-related industry forms the core of the major. The management of public lands and waters is a related interest. Technical aspects of agriculture are intensely analyzed, since the ability to create practical solutions and get results are the intended outcomes of the degree. Marketing and business management are also important learning areas.

Plan of Study
The plan of study usually shares the same core courses as an agricultural sciences major, including biology, chemistry, physics, and mathematics. The curriculum progresses to agricultural production, economic analysis, futures market analysis, world economics, and production forecasting. Field trips involving close-up study of working farms to analyze agricultural business decisions and policy-making practices are included.

Expect to Take
Chemistry I and II with lab, biology with lab, calculus I and II, economics of farm/ranch production, agricultural marketing, price analysis, land-use planning, statistical methods.

Suggested High School Subjects
Advanced mathematics, advanced science, economics, college-preparatory business electives, computer studies.

General Interest Areas
Science, agriculture, economics, statistics, mathematical analysis, business.

Some Career Possibilities

agricultural agent	agricultural engineer	economic analyst
financial analyst	forester	range manager
agricultural economist	agronomist	farmer/rancher
food and drug inspector	lawyer	teacher

Some Related Majors

agronomy	business administration	soils and water
animal sciences	business economics	management
environmental science	ecology	
marketing	plant sciences	

AGRONOMY

Description
Agronomy is the study of soils and crop production. As a specialty within the broader area of agriculture, it focuses on the experimental and research analysis of crop plants, the factors that affect yield, plant and crop diseases, and varieties of crops and their cultivation in relation to climate variation and soil quality. In addition, agronomy is concerned with the improvement of special-purpose plants such as turf grasses for home lawns.

Plan of Study
The plan of study emphasizes the agricultural sciences such as plant physiology, horticulture, and ecology. Coursework also includes basic sciences such as chemistry, biology, and botany. Field work with professors and the conducting of experiments on soil samples or related activities are significant features of the undergraduate program.

Expect to Take
Biology, botany, general chemistry, calculus with differential equations, organic chemistry, plant anatomy, plant nutrition, biochemistry, soil conservation, silviculture.

Suggested High School Subjects
Advanced science through biology and chemistry, advanced mathematics, computer studies.

General Interest Areas
Agriculture, science, mathematics, research.

Some Career Possibilities
agronomist	military officer	technical writer
laboratory technician	college professor	government or
biochemist	quality control	research scientist
management trainee	technician	
biologist	food and drug inspector	

Some Related Majors
agricultural business/economics	animal sciences	soils/water man.
environmental engineering	geography	botany
forestry	biology	ecology

AMERICAN STUDIES

Description
American studies traces the development of the United States as a nation, from a multidisciplinary frame of reference. History, culture, economics, sociology, and literature all play a role in the study of America and its people. Readings and/or projects in these areas foster an understanding of how American society functions. This broad, flexible approach provides students with a valuable background for a wide array of careers in the private and public sectors, since the skills developed include observation, analysis, planning, and creative thinking for the community and workplace.

Plan of Study
The program of study may involve a concentration in one or more areas under the American studies umbrella. Beginning with a core curriculum of courses intended to provide a broad foundation of knowledge, the student may elect to specialize, during the junior and senior years, in such areas as U.S. history and society, women's studies, culture and communications. Special projects, seminars in topics of current importance, and independent research will complete the major.

Expect to Take
Introduction to U.S. history, American political and social thought, history of the mass media, the American people, sex, race, and class in American literature.

Suggested High School Subjects
Advanced English, advanced social studies, foreign language, computer literacy.

General Interest Areas
Writing, politics, humanities.

Some Career Possibilities
book/magazine editor	government area	political analyst
college professor	specialist	public admin.
foreign service officer	lawyer	secondary teacher
freelance writer	military officer	social worker

Some Related Majors
communications	media study	sociology
history	political science	urban studies
journalism	secondary education	

ANALYTICAL CHEMISTRY

Description
Analytical chemistry is a branch of the chemical sciences that studies the relationship between the physical structure of material and its chemical composition. Observation and measurement of materials are the principal methods of the study; the design and improvement of instruments and techniques for conducting the observations is yet another area within this major. Colorimetry and x-ray crystallography are some of the tools of the analytical chemist.

Plan of Study
The plan of study emphasizes firm grounding in physics, chemistry, and advanced math. Upper-division work entails specialty courses in the major, extensive laboratory-based study in topics of current interest, and independent supervised research. Students interested in the major should seek an accredited program.

Expect to Take
Chemistry I, II, and III with lab, physics I and II with lab, calculus I and II, organic chemistry I and II, chemical instrumentation lab, intermediate analytical chemistry, experimental techniques, senior research, internships.

Suggested High School Subjects
Advanced science, advanced mathematics, computer studies.

General Interest Areas
Science, chemistry, research, independent analysis, mathematical/scientific modeling.

Some Career Possibilities
analytical chemist	college professor	general chemist
industrial chemist	medical analyst	research chemist
biochemist	entrepreneur	geochemist
laboratory technician	pharmacologist	technical writer

Some Related Majors
biochemistry	medical technology	geochemistry
inorganic chemistry	chemistry	physical chemistry
chemical engineering	pharmacy	geology

ANATOMY

Description
This is the study of the body structure and proportions of humans and other animals. Weight ratios, analysis of bone growth and development, and study of internal organs and systems as they relate to bone structure, size, and shape are all elements of this major. Anatomy as a major is available in only a small number of undergraduate institutions in America. The student interested in pursuing this field directly after high school will have to search carefully for the college that offers a true major in anatomy. Students often study anatomy in anticipation of admission to medical school. In this case, the specific field of interest is called "Human Anatomy." Similarly, for those desiring to attend schools of veterinary medicine as a graduate study, the undergraduate major could be "Comparative Anatomy."

Plan of Study
The plan of study for this major consists of a very strong emphasis on the sciences, beginning with biology, through anatomy, physiology, and the detailed study of the nine systems of the body, and on to laboratory chemistry and several courses in mathematics.

Expect to Take
Anatomy and physiology, general chemistry, organic chemistry, calculus with differential equations, structures of invertebrates, structures of vertebrates, skeletal systems, circulatory systems, digestive systems.

Suggested High School Subjects
Advanced science through biology and physics, advanced mathematics through calculus (AP preferred), computer studies.

General Interest Areas
Science, mathematics, medicine, research.

Some Career Possibilities

anatomist	embalmer	physical therapist
biologist	laboratory technician	physician
biomedical engineer	medical assistant	physiologist
college professor	microbiologist	technical writer

Some Related Majors

animal sciences	embryology	speech path./aud.
anthropology	human/animal	zoology
bioengineering	physiology	
biology	organic chemistry	

ANIMAL SCIENCES

Description
Animal Sciences is generally concerned with the care and feeding of livestock and poultry. The major includes the study of breeding, feeding, and management of beef and dairy e, sheep, swine, horses, and poultry. A focus of the major is the improvement of the quality of the herd(s), as well as to provide sufficient quantity of product to meet the ebb and flow of demand. The curriculum may also be titled "Animal Husbandry," "Animal Industries," "Avian Science," or "Animal Agriculture."

Plan of Study
The plan of study begins with extensive coursework in biology, chemistry, physics, and advanced mathematics. At the upper-division level, the student may pursue courses in a chosen area of specialization, together with professional studies in related industries, to form a coherent program leading to the B.S. degree. B.A. degree candidates also may take courses in business organization and management to complete the major. Internships and/or supervised independent study in selected topics may be included.

Expect to Take
Biology I and II with lab, chemistry I and II, calculus I and II, animal industry, animal genetics, feeds and feeding, breeds and registry associations, physiology of reproduction, livestock management.

Suggested High School Subjects
Advanced science, advanced mathematics, computer studies, selected college-preparatory business electives.

General Interest Areas
Science, animal husbandry, farming.

Some Career Possibilities
agronomist	bacteriologist	livestock manager
animal breeder	college professor	racetrack manager
animal researcher	ecologist	teacher
animal scientist	farmer/rancher	technical writer

Some Related Majors
agricultural business/economics	biology	human/animal
agronomy	embryology	marine biology
anatomy	genetics	marketing zoology

ANTHROPOLOGY

Description
Anthropology is the study of humans-their varied physical and cultural characteristics, distribution, customs and social relationships. Important areas of concern within the discipline include the evolution of human beings, the development of early cultures, and diversity of cultural development among peoples as well as their political systems religious practices and value systems Anthropology as offered in four-year undergraduate programs is often divided into subspecialties such as physical anthropology, cultural anthropology, or linguistics Otherwise, anthropology may be coupled with area studies majors such as African or Asian studies

Plan of Study
The plan of study begins with introductory courses in the sophomore year, followed by intensive technical study that incorporates each of the principal subdivisions mentioned above. Students opt for a specialty in one of these areas through the junior and senior years, ending with field experiences, seminars in topics of current importance, and supervised independent research.

Expect to Take
College algebra, introduction to anthropology, cultural development, physical anthropology, cultural ecology, peoples of Asia or the African desert, religious customs of the world, medical anthropology, dental anthropology, seminar in cultural linguistics, field research, independent research internships, field excursions to on-site "digs".

Suggested High School Subjects
Advanced social studies advanced science including biology and physics foreign language, computer studies, electives related to anthropology

General Interest Areas
Social science, biology, history

Some Career Possibilities
archaeologist	linguistic anthropologist	editor/writer
historian	physical anthropologist	geologist
college professor	cultural anthropologist	

Some Related Majors
African Studies	paleontology	sociology
history	archaeology	behavioral sci.
Native American cultural	psychology	
studies	area studies	

APPLIED MATHEMATICS

Description
Applied mathematics is the study and use of mathematical algorithms and procedures for the solution of real-world problems. The major is divided into three concentrations: physical sciences, operations research, and statistics/probability.
Each concentration contains a specific body of courses, selected with the help of a departmental advisor and intended to prepare the student for a range of careers in business, government, private enterprise, research, and teaching. As with many other math/science majors, the B.S. degree is the preferred preparation for graduate study. In the B.A. program, this major may be combined with teaching certification.

Plan of Study
The plan of study emphasizes such basic background as college algebra, calculus, and numerical analysis at the lower-division level, then proceeds to topics such as mathematical modeling, graph theory, topology, and actuarial mathematics.

Expect to Take
Differential equations, number systems, linear algebra, mathematical logic, operations research, complex variables, applied algebra, geometry, special topics, independent study and research.

Suggested High School Subjects
Advanced mathematics through calculus, science through chemistry and physics, computer studies.

General Interest Areas
Mathematics, problem solving, data analysis.

Some Career Possibilities

actuary	college professor	economist
lawyer	research scientist	technical writer
applied mathematician	computer programmer	financial analyst
operations researcher	systems analyst	

Some Related Majors

accounting	economics	business statistics
computer science	business economics	systems analysis
banking/finance	operations research	

ARCHAEOLOGY

Description
This is the scientific study of culture through the use of relics, ruins, and other remains. Often excavation or other field activities are necessary to gather information for examination. By reconstructing the past, a picture is formed of what life might have been like in other ages of human existence. This calls for a fascination with history and culture. For data gathering, the archaeologist also uses physical science technology such as dating methods, cartography, and geology.

Plan of Study
The program of study is sometimes included as a concentration within an anthropology major or coupled with a program in art or art history. A core curriculum of courses in classical archaeology, archaeological methods and observation techniques leads to courses in advanced methods, seminars on current topics, and directed research.

Expect to Take
Introduction to archaeology, archaeology of classical civilizations, archaeological field methods, statistics, computer science for the archaeologist.

Suggested High School Subjects
Advanced social studies, earth science, advanced mathematics, computer studies.

General Interest Areas
Science, social studies.

Some Career Possibilities

lawyer	paleontologist	technical writer
archaeologist	research scientist	editor
museum curator	college professor	anthropologist
archivist	teacher	biologist

Some Related Majors

African studies	history	area studies
classics	paleontology	behavioral sci.
Native American cultural	anthropology	
studies	psychology	

ARCHITECTURE

Description
Architecture, a skill which dates back to the earliest civilizations, is the art and science of erecting structures. It is viewed as being functional and technological as well as esthetic, and it entails knowledge of structural stability, construction materials, and techniques for the styling and design of buildings. Architecture, while an important major of study in its own right at the graduate level, is often viewed as an interdisciplinary study at the undergraduate level, coupled with coursework in art and design as part of a fine arts program.

Plan of Study
The plan of study provides an introduction to the discipline of design and includes opportunities to practice actual physical planning techniques as well. Internships with professional architects, either within the scope of study or as independent study projects outside the normal school year, also may be available.

Expect to Take
Introductory drawing, architectural design, computer-aided design and drafting, building science and technology, architectural analysis and criticism, engineering graphics, surveying, urban environment and structures.

Suggested High School Subjects
Advanced mathematics, advanced art, mechanical/architectural drawing, computer aided design (CAD), foreign language.

General Interest Areas
Art, design, construction, mathematics.

Some Career Possibilities
architect	college professor	museum curator
architectural draftsman	consultant	public admin.
art teacher	industrial designer	technical writer
auto designer	landscape architect	urban planner

Some Related Majors
archaeology	fine arts	naval architecture
civil engineering	interior design	urban studies
electrical engineering	landscape architecture	

AREA STUDIES

Description

Area studies is a social science—or social studies-based curriculum—that focuses on investigating one or more geographic regions of the world. This is usually presented as an interdisciplinary study, in that coursework in the major covers all significant aspects of the area under study including politics, culture, religion, economics, and literature. Fluency in one of the languages of the area of interest is advantageous and language courses should therefore be included as electives.

Plan of Study

The plan of study emphasizes work in the topics enumerated above. Additional studies include the disciplines of anthropology, comparative literature, history of the area, and sociology. Some colleges combine this major with teacher education and certification courses; others urge students to consider area studies as a springboard to graduate study in political science, international relations, or law.

Expect to Take

Peoples, culture, literature, and history of the area, economics, politics, and religions, introduction to anthropology, cultural anthropology, at least one foreign language.

Suggested High School Subjects

Advanced English, advanced social studies, foreign language study, computer literacy.

General Interest Areas

History, social science, language.

Some Career Possibilities

college professor	government area	political analyst
editor	specialist	public admin.
foreign service officer	lawyer	teacher
freelance writer	military officer	technical writer

Some Related Majors

African studies	anthropology	political science
Native American cultural	archaeology	sociology
studies	history	
American studies	international relations	

ART EDUCATION

Description
This education specialty is designed to provide students with a fundamental understanding of fine arts for the purpose of instructing others. The prospective art teacher will have experience in all forms of art, including painting, commercial art, fashion design. sculpting, and other traditional and contemporary art forms. Specialization in one form is possible for the college- or university-level teacher; elementary and secondary school teachers, on the other hand, are usually generalists in the field.

Plan of Study
The plan of study encompasses a broad exposure to all aspects of art: two-dimensional studio art, drawing, and painting, as well as three-dimensional work in ceramics and sculpture. Art history, art criticism and evaluation techniques will also be included.

Expect to Take
Design foundations, drawing I and II, art history, watercolor painting, ceramics, printmaking, commercial graphic design, art survey, medieval art, student teaching.

Suggested High School Subjects
Advanced mathematics and science, computer studies, art electives and art seminars.

General Interest Areas
Teaching, drawing, design

Some Career Possibilities
art restorer	book illustrator	commercial artist
fashion designer	medical illustrator	secondary teacher
artist	college professor	elementary teacher
interior designer	museum archivist	

Some Related Majors
architecture	cinematography	secondary ed.
art history/appreciation	communications	fashion merch.
environmental design	dramatic arts	interior design

ART HISTORY AND APPRECIATION

Description
This major consists of the study of art in all its various forms, from earliest times to the present day. It emphasizes the development of art through the centuries, the relationship of artistic expression with the historical period in which it is produced, and the ability to evaluate and compare works of art.

Plan of Study
The plan of study is an extensive one, beginning with general academic core courses interspersed with open electives in art appreciation and history. At the upper-division level, the student is encouraged to focus on one world region for intensive art study. In many programs, students have options to study more than one geographical region or historical period to achieve more breadth of expertise. An occasional program may offer a concentration in art appraisal, requiring courses such as methodology of appraisal and other related subjects.

Expect to Take
Introduction to art history, medieval art, tribal art, Italian Renaissance art, modern architecture, readings in art history.

Suggested High School Subjects
Advanced art (especially canvas work), advanced social studies, history electives, art history electives, computer literacy.

General Interest Areas
Art, art history, history.

Some Career Possibilities

art appraiser	museum curator	teacher
college professor	art historian	artist
commercial artist	sales representative	technical writer
art critic	art restorer	cartoonist

Some Related Majors

fashion merchandising	interior design	secondary ed.
archaeology	art education	enviro. design
fine arts	landscape architecture	
architecture	classics	

ASTRONOMY

Description
The major in astronomy examines the motion and nature of the sun, moon, stars, planets and
the celestial bodies. Astronomy brings to bear the knowledge of the mathematician, the
chemist, and the physicist. Astronomy has evolved through recent centuries from an
observational science, relying on data gathered from peering through a telescope to an
experimental science, including space exploration.

Plan of Study
Some colleges offer astronomy as an individual major. More frequently, program offerings
are titled "Physics and Astronomy," "Astronomy/Planetary Sciences," or "Astrophysics." This
underscores the close alliance of astronomy with physics in today's colleges and emphasizes
the sophisticated grounding in physics required of astronomers. The plan of study consists of
courses in general physics with lab, chemistry, electromagnetics, and core courses in
astronomy. A close working relationship with a faculty advisor is very important when
pursuing a major in astronomy.

Expect to Take
Physics I-IV, basic mechanics, electricity and magnetism, relativity seminar, astronomy I and
II, astrophysics.

Suggested High School Subjects
Advanced science, advanced mathematics, computer studies.

General Interest Areas
Science, mathematics.

Some Career Possibilities
astronomer	climatologist	computer scientist
government researcher	physicist	freelance writer
astrophysicist	college professor	secondary teacher
meteorologist	research scientist	technical writer

Some Related Majors
aerospace engineering	astrophysics	geophysics
applied mathematics	geochemistry	earth sciences
ecology	chemistry	physics

ASTROPHYSICS

Description
This major combines the study of astronomy with that of physics in a field devoted to the exploration of laws of physics which affect astronomical bodies, their relationships with one another, and the discovery of clues to the origin and development of the universe.

Plan of Study
The plan of study is a challenging one. At the undergraduate level, the focus is on the in depth study of topics in physics, with particular emphasis on such areas as mechanics, quantum theory, electromagnetism, and electricity. This is supplemented with a heavy concentration in advanced mathematics and electives in astronomy. A B.A. degree is available in this major; the B.S. is preferred, especially for students intending to pursue the Ph.D. in astrophysics. A close working relationship with a faculty advisor is crucial to the successful completion of this program.

Expect to Take
Physics I-IV with lab; calculus and advanced calculus, chemistry I and II; modern astronomy; introduction to astrophysics, galaxies, quasars, and the universe; electricity and magnetism; computer studies.

Suggested High School Subjects
Advanced science, advanced mathematics, computer science.

General Interest Areas
Science, mathematics, earth and space sciences.

Some Career Possibilities
astronomer	climatologist	comp. specialist
government researcher	physicist	technical writer
astrophysicist	college professor	freelance writer
meteorologist	research scientist	

Some Related Majors
aerospace engineering	geophysics	earth sciences
geochemistry	astronomy	physics
applied mathematics	mathematics	ecology

BACTERIOLOGY

Description
This major studies a branch of microbiology that concerns the examination of bacteria and their classification by type, as well as the analysis of their physiological and biochemical properties. The bacteriologist researches bacteria that are suspect in causing human disease and studies the ecological significance of bacteria in the cycle of matter.

Plan of Study
The plan of study involves research in experimental biology, molecular biology, and selected topics in the causes of human disease. It also includes ecological virus research. independent research in a particular area under the direct supervision of a faculty member, the study of cell analysis, and differentiation and development of cells.

Expect to Take
Biology with lab, biochemistry, bacteriology, microbial physiology, organic chemistry, genetics, probability and statistics, calculus I and II.

Suggested High School Subjects
Advanced science including biology (AP preferred), advanced mathematics including pre-calculus and calculus, computer science.

General Interest Areas
Sciences, mathematics, experimentation/research, independent study, analysis.

Some Career Possibilities
bacteriologist	researcher	government tech
microbiologist	college professor	zoologist
biochemist	textbook writer	medical sales
parasitologist	embryologist	representative
biologist	veterinarian	

Some Related Majors
anatomy	biology	cytology
embryology	botany	microbiology
biochemistry	marine	toxicology
histology	biology	

BANKING AND FINANCE

Description
Banking and finance is usually an area of concentration within a general business, business administration, or business studies curriculum. It includes the process of funding and operating a business and the methods of attracting capital investment, the management of income versus debt satisfaction, the development of financial statements, and the general use of money for underwriting the expense of business.

Plan of Study
The plan of study includes coursework in business operations, management, accounting, and sales and marketing techniques, as well as work in corporate finance, international finance, and business statistics. Some colleges also provide a cooperative work-experience program in which students function as employees, learning job skills in a business environment.

Expect to Take
Introduction to business, principles of accounting, money and banking, taxation I and II, auditing, labor economics, securities analysis, financial statements.

Suggested High School Subjects
Advanced mathematics, computer studies, business electives such as business law and accounting

General Interest Areas
Mathematics, business, law.

Some Career Possibilities
accountant	business enterprise	real estate broker
bank manager	officer	sales rep.
budget officer	comptroller	treasurer
business education teacher	loan officer	claims adjuster

Some Related Majors
accounting	business statistics	international bus.
business administration	computer science	marketing op.
business economics	economics	research

BEHAVIORAL SCIENCES

Description
This major is the study of a group of sciences that specialize in some aspect of human behavior, whether manifested in individual acts between persons or in actions between, or among, groups of persons. As an undergraduate major, it is largely a survey area; that is, students use it as preparation for graduate study in one of the behavioral sciences such as psychology, sociology, anthropology, linguistics, or the communication/information sciences.

Plan of Study
The plan of study is broad and varied. Humanities courses predominate at the lower-division level, with some opportunity to take behavioral science electives. At the upper-division level, the coursework spans the behavioral sciences, with the senior year devoted to concentration on a specialty. Supervised independent research in that area and field experience may be included.

Expect to Take
Social psychology, organizational psychology, statistics for behavioral sciences, behavioral research, perception, cognition, survey data analysis, biopsychology, personality and psychopathology.

Suggested High School Subjects
English including advanced reading and writing skills, advanced social studies, foreign language, computer studies.

General Interest Areas
Psychology, sociology, anthropology.

Some Career Possibilities
anthropologist	government employee	public health
biologist	management consultant	sociologist
clergy	military officer	technical writer
college professor	psychologist	lawyer

Some Related Majors
anthropology	educational psychology	social psych.
clinical psychology	marketing	social sciences
clinical social work	psychology	sociology

BIBLE STUDIES

Description
The Bible studies major examines and analyses the books of the Bible, both Old and New Testaments. In addition, this major examines the works of commentators and authors who attempt to interpret the meaning or communicate an understanding of the Bible. Generally, this major is pursued by those who intend to teach, preach, or write about the Bible, often as ministers of a religious group. Occasionally, laypeople interested in the study of the Bible for its own sake will select this major.

Plan of Study
The plan of study may include a core curriculum of liberal arts or general studies during the first two years, with electives in one or more classical languages such as Latin, Greek, or Hebrew. Later, coursework specializes in the study of individual books of the Bible, Bible history, and Bible exegesis, as well as individual research projects and advanced seminars. Field experiences may be required, including research trips to the lands where the Bible was written, teaching or preaching assignments, and direct work with a congregation.

Expect to Take
Beginning/intermediate Latin, Greek, and Hebrew, origins of the Bible, the Pentateuch, understanding Genesis, the Book of Job, Old Testament exegesis, the New Testament as history, modern scripture scholarship, independent research, seminars in current topics, speech.

Suggested High School Subjects
Advanced social studies, foreign languages, computer studies, literature electives such as "Bible as Literature."

General Interest Areas
Religion, public speaking, social work, ancient history, research.

Some Career Possibilities
college professor	lawyer	missionary
psychologist	school official	theological writer
counselor	minister	priest
rabbi	teacher	therapist

Some Related Majors
classics	psychology	theological studies
philosophy	English	foreign languages
communications	secondary education	

BIOCHEMISTRY

Description
Biochemistry is a study that combines the life processes in terms of chemical reactions within living cells. The subdivisions within this field include metabolism, the study of the chemical changes through which organisms obtain the energy to develop and reproduce, and descriptive biochemistry, which analyzes cell structures to determine how they adapt and survive.

Plan of Study
The plan of study requires strong preparation in appropriate sciences and mathematics the first two years of college. Usually, application is then made for admission to the upper division major. Academic advisement during the first two years is critical, since at many colleges biochemistry is a limited-enrollment program.

Expect to Take
Biology I and II with lab, general, organic, and physical chemistry, physics I and II with lab, calculus and advanced calculus, kinetics, spectrophotometry.

Suggested High School Subjects
Advanced science including biology and chemistry, advanced mathematics including calculus, computer studies. AP courses preferred.

General Interest Areas
Science, mathematics, research.

Some Career Possibilities

assayer	biologist	college professor
government researcher	microbiologist	consultant
biochemist	chemist	research scientist
laboratory technician	pharmacologist	technical writer

Some Related Majors

analytical chemistry	botany	embryology
bacteriology	chemical engineering	genetics
biology	chemistry	
biophysics	cytology	

BIOENGINEERING/ BIOMEDICAL ENGINEERING

Description
The terms above are used interchangeably to describe the study of the application of engineering knowledge to the fields of medicine and biology. A relatively new field, bioengineering combines design engineering and biological knowledge to create devices, design operations, and invent techniques to prolong or improve the health and well-being of humans and animals. Bioengineering includes the development of prosthetic devices used to replace lost or nonfunctioning parts of the body, dialysis methodologies, hip and knee implantations, and techniques for vascular bypass surgery.

Plan of Study
The plan of study follows the structure of all engineering programs, with physics, chemistry, calculus, and engineering sciences at the lower-division level and more engineering coursework and supervised research at the upper-division level. In some colleges, the bioengineering or biomedical specialty is an augment to a major in a traditional engineering area, such as mechanical, civil, electrical, or chemical. Coursework in physiology, corrosion, corrosion fatigue, signal acquisition and transmission, and modeling of physiological systems is stressed. Independent, supervised projects in current topics are required.

Expect to Take
Physics I-III, chemistry I and II with lab, calculus, engineering mechanics, thermodynamics, electrical circuitry, materials science, design project I and II, bioelectric and biocontrol systems, process engineering.

Suggested High School Subjects
Advanced science through physics, advanced mathematics through calculus, social studies, foreign language, computer studies.

General Interest Areas
Mathematics, science, medicine, research, human systems, analysis of data.

Some Career Possibilities
bioengineer	college professor	research scientist
medical consultant	physiologist	materials eng.
biomedical engineer	lawyer	mechanical eng.
physician	reliability engineer	

Some Related Majors
engineering	biology	mechanical eng.
physics	human/animal	biophysics
anatomy	physiology	physics

BIOLOGY, GENERAL

Description
Biology is the science of living systems. It examines the nature, structure, function, and living organisms. Biology is inherently interdisciplinary, requiring knowledge of a variety of physical sciences and mathematics. As an undergraduate major, biology or its companion field, biological science, is appropriate preparation for the study of medicine or other health-related professions.

Plan of Study
The plan of study involves extensive work in laboratory biology, chemistry, and physics, as well as mathematics through advanced calculus. In addition, supplemental work may be included in specialized subjects such as microbiology, cell biology, and plant biology, depending on the area of emphasis in which the college's biology department is strongest.

Expect to Take
Biology I–III with lab, physical chemistry, organic chemistry, general physics with lab, calculus, advanced calculus, statistics, anatomy and physiology, field studies, seminars.

Suggested High School Subjects
Advanced science including biology (AP preferred), advanced mathematics, computer studies.

General Interest Areas
Science, mathematics, research, medicine, health-related careers.

Some Career Possibilities

biologist	lawyer	physicist
chemist	marine biologist	secondary teacher
college professor	microbiologist	veterinarian
ecologist	physician	zoologist

Some Related Majors

anatomy	biochemistry	botany
animal sciences	bioengineering	genetics
bacteriology	biophysics	human/an phys.

BIOPHYSICS

Description
This is a branch of physics specializing in the study of living organisms. It analyzes life processes from the point of view of the laws of physics and physical chemistry. Quantitative analysis and research are at the core of this major. Occasionally incorporated within the department of medicine, it is an upper-division curriculum; admission is determined by an evaluation of preparation during the first two years. As with other highly specialized programs described in this book, close advisement by a faculty member is required.

Plan of Study
The plan of study in biophysics is quite rigorous. At the lower-division level, general physics I and II, chemistry of various types, advanced calculus, and selected specialized electives are mandatory. In addition, research projects and laboratory experiences are evaluated for adherence to correct research methods, as well as for the ability to identify areas for future research.

Expect to Take
Introduction to biophysics, organic chemistry, physical chemistry, statistical mechanics, problems in biophysics, thermodynamics, spectroscopic techniques.

Suggested High School Subjects
Advanced science through biology and physics (AP preferred), computer studies.

General Interest Areas
Science, mathematics, research, experimentation.

Some Career Possibilities

aerospace engineer	biologist	college professor
health physicist	nuclear physicist	secondary teacher
astrophysicist	biophysicist	consultant
laboratory technician	research scientist	

Some Related Majors

biochemistry	biology	cytology
genetics	human/animal	embryology
bioengineering	physiology	
histology	physics	

BOTANY, GENERAL

Description
Botany is the study of plants, especially their structure and development. This major also concerns the diversity and variety of plant life, evolutionary relationships among plants, the functional systems within plants (physiology), and environmental relationships among plants as well as between plant life and animal life. Botany also may include some background in plant diseases, soil factors, conservation methods, and related topics.

Plan of Study
The plan of study emphasizes topics in biology and chemistry with appropriate laboratory experiences at the lower-division level, as well as stressing the study of mathematics through calculus. At the upper-division level, considerable time is dedicated to such topics as plant anatomy and physiology, genus and species of plants, and the distribution and characteristics of plants by region. Research and supervised study of current topics in botany, as well as an internship experience in a research setting, complete the course of study.

Expect to Take
Biology I–III with lab, chemistry I and II with lab, calculus I (possibly II), taxonomy of plants, plant anatomy, physiology with lab, plant systematics, plant geography, ecology of plants.

Suggested High School Subjects
Advanced science through biology and chemistry, advanced mathematics through calculus, computer studies.

General Interest Areas
Science, mathematics, plant life, experimentation, field research, data analysis.

Some Career Possibilities

agronomist	ecologist	research scientist
archaeologist	laboratory technician	soil scientist
botanist	paleontologist	technical writer
college professor	plant physiologist	

Some Related Majors

agronomy	embryology	microbiology
bacteriology	entomology	organic chemistry
biology	marine biology	paleontology

BUSINESS ADMINISTRATION

Description
Business administration is the study of the techniques and skills needed to operate a business. Since executive decision-making is based on having some knowledge of every area of operations, coursework includes all aspects of business, including business organization, production, sales and marketing, accounting, and personnel administration. A business administration major may concentrate in one of the above areas, focusing on a specific facet of business while taking courses in the remaining areas to complete the program. Also known as "Business Management."

Plan of Study
Colleges with a strong business department may offer a dual major together with such studies as economics, international business, business law, or operations research. Since a large number of colleges offer this major in some form, the reader is urged to study and compare catalogs carefully to find the program best suited to one's goals.

Expect to Take
Introduction to business, principles of accounting, management techniques, business law, finance, principles of marketing, microeconomics, human resources management.

Suggested High School Subjects
Advanced social studies, mathematics through algebra, computer studies, college-preparatory business electives.

General Interest Areas
Business, law, mathematics.

Some Career Possibilities
real estate broker	business education	manager
stock broker accountant	teacher	market researcher
administrative assistant	comptroller	
contract administrator	economist	

Some Related Majors
accounting	business economics	marketing op.
advertising	business statistics	research
agricultural business/economics	economics	real estate

BUSINESS ECONOMICS

Description
Business economics is an area of concentration within business administration or general business. It concerns the quantitative analysis of business trends and so-called "cycles". This entails the investigation of
the forces that affect the rise and fall of business activity. The impact of this activity on employment, capital outlay, investment, and profit/loss is examined. The major is geared heavily toward statistical analysis, so a strong background in mathematics is a necessity.

Plan of Study
The plan of study involves an in-depth exposure to economics and a core of courses from the business or business administration department, many of which will concern accounting or finance. Some colleges award a dual major in business and economics upon completion; those that do not, offer business economics as a formal major can prepare a student for this career through appropriate faculty advisement.

Expect to Take
Introduction to business, accounting I and II, macroeconomics, microeconomics, cost accounting, managerial economics, money and banking, finance, budgeting, business statistics I and II.

Suggested High School Subjects
Advanced social studies, economics, advanced mathematics including calculus, computer studies, college-preparatory business electives.

General Interest Areas
Business, statistics, mathematics.

Some Career Possibilities

accountant (C.P.A.)	cost accountant	manager
budget officer	economist	market analyst
business economist	government employee	sales rep.
comptroller	lawyer	treasurer

Some Related Majors

accounting	computer science	marketing
business administration	economics	mathematics
business statistics	international business	operations res.

BUSINESS EDUCATION

Description
This major is the study of business and entrepreneurship in all its forms, as preparation for teaching the full range of business courses to secondary school students. Business education majors develop a thorough background in secretarial practice, accounting, office management, marketing, and distributive education. Student teaching experiences and seminars on current topics culminate in eligibility for teaching certification.

Plan of Study
The plan of study begins with a core curriculum of general studies in the lower-division level, supplemented by electives in business education. Upper-division students pursue advanced work in business topics such as typing, shorthand, law, marketing and sales, and distributive education. Studies leading to eligibility for teacher certification will be capped by student teaching experiences and seminars in current topics in the field.

Expect to Take
Typing I and II, shorthand I and II, accounting I and II, business law, principles of marketing, macroeconomics, statistics, computers in business, income tax accounting, auditing, methods of teaching business, seminars.

Suggested High School Subjects
Advanced mathematics, social studies, computer studies, business electives.

General Interest Areas
Business, teaching, entrepreneurship.

Some Career Possibilities
accountant	business owner	proprietary school
auditor	executive secretary	instructor
business consultant	paralegal specialist	sales rep.
business manager		secondary teacher

Some Related Majors
accounting	business statistics	research
applied mathematics	economics	secondary ed.
banking/finance	labor/industrial relations	
business economics	marketing operations	

BUSINESS STATISTICS

Description
A highly specialized major within the department of business administration, business statistics examines the techniques for the collection and use of empirical information in making business decisions. The focus is on the design and analysis of surveys, industrial research, and the conduct of experimental business programs and market research. Frequently titled "Statistical Analysis," the study usually includes extensive computer science and business information-processing courses.

Plan of Study
The plan of study begins with core courses for business majors, with electives in basic statistical methods. A firm grounding in theoretical higher mathematics and advanced statistics and probability leads to work in descriptive statistics, graphic methods, hypothesis testing, and interpretation of confidence intervals. Management courses in policy planning and decision making are also incorporated.

Expect to Take
Quantitative decision making for business statistical methods, sampling theory, analysis of variance system simulation, statistics of market research, calculus I-III.
market analyst operations researcher statistical accountant.

Suggested High School Subjects
Advanced mathematics including calculus, advanced science, computer studies, selected college-preparatory business electives, statistics electives.

General Interest Areas
Mathematics, business, statistics research, independent analysis.

Some Career Possibilities
business statistician	comptroller	teacher
manager	lawyer	consultant
college professor	management analyst	

Some Related Majors
accounting	business administration	economics
applied mathematics	business economics	insurance mark.
banking/finance	computer science	systems analysis

CHEMICAL ENGINEERING

Description
Chemical engineering is the study of materials, chemicals, or compounds that make processes work, or fill production specifications or needs. The chemical engineer studies the effects of chemicals or compounds on one another and seeks ways to ameliorate or reverse undesirable effects. Another aim is the discovery of new, more advanced chemicals or compounds. Knowledge of the principles of heat transfer, flow of fluids, filtration processes, distillation, extraction, fermentation, and chemical kinetics are but a few of the chemical engineer's skills.

Plan of Study
The plan of study typically begins with two years of foundation in physics, chemistry (both organic and physical), mathematics through advanced calculus, and occasional engineering topics. At the upper-division level, intense work in the various topics mentioned above is emphasized, culminating in the final semesters with guided projects and laboratory opportunities under the supervision of faculty members.

Expect to Take
Concepts of engineering, physical mechanics, thermodynamics, electricity and magnetism, engineering lab I-IV, chemical process engineering, chemical engineering seminar, guided projects.

Suggested High School Subjects
Advanced mathematics including calculus, advanced science through physics, computer studies.

General Interest Areas
Mathematics, chemistry, experimentation, data analysis, research.

Some Career Possibilities
chemical engineer	management consultant	research scientist
chemist	metallurgist	technical writer
college professor	petroleum engineer	
lawyer	plastics engineer	

Some Related Majors
chemistry	metallurgical	petroleum eng.
industrial engineering	engineering	physics
inorganic chemistry	mining engineering	
mechanical engineering	organic chemistry	

CHEMISTRY, GENERAL

Description
This is the study of the various kinds, composition, structure, and properties of mar and the changes which it undergoes through the action of other matter and forces. The study of chemistry is important in such fields as medicine, engineering, scientific search, and the environment. As an autonomous science, it is divided into several subspecialties including analytical, inorganic, organic, and physical chemistry; each is described as a major field of study elsewhere in this book.

Plan of Study
The plan of study is nearly identical among institutions offering the chemistry major. Foundation courses in chemistry, physics, and advanced mathematics occupy the first two years of study. At the upper-division level, students work on a specific concentration, culminating in supervised, independent research projects and selected internship opportunities. The candidate for the B.S. degree may pursue a graduate degree in the concentration or move on to medicine, dentistry, or another health-related field. A student pursuing the B.A. in chemistry will be exposed to a more general background in the field, with a view toward secondary school teaching or careers such as law. Dual-major programs can be developed, with faculty advisement, in areas as diverse as business administration or chemical instrumentation.

Expect to Take
Physics I and II with lab, general chemistry I and II with lab, organic chemistry I and II, inorganic chemistry I and II, experimental chemistry, calculus I and II, and independent research.

Suggested High School Subjects
Advanced mathematics, advanced science through physics, computer studies.

General Interest Areas
Science, mathematics, research.

Some Career Possibilities
chemical engineer	general chemist	pharmacist
chemical researcher	geochemist	teacher
college professor	geologist	technical writer

Some Related Majors
analytical chemistry	geochemistry	pharmacy
biochemistry	inorganic chemistry	physical chemistry
chemical engineering	organic chemistry	public health

CINEMATOGRAPHY

Description
Cinematography is the study of the art of motion picture photography and, as a major, is concerned with the production of films rather than with film criticism or film history, though the study of these areas is incorporated into the curriculum. In some colleges, this program is titled "Film Studies"; in others, it is considered part of the wider communications major.

Plan of Study
The plan of study begins with two years of work in a core curriculum of academic courses, interspersed with courses that span the range of the communications arts. The junior and senior years offer intermediate and advanced courses in communications, as well as film production techniques which are viewed and critiqued by the professor. Students' filmmaking projects often arise from the students' current interests, developed from the study of many other films and from courses that emphasize particular aspects of the filmmaker's craft. Externship experiences and the production of film projects are integral parts of the major.

Expect to Take
History of motion pictures, fundamentals of filmmaking, film theory and technique, cinema writing, film direction and production, production workshop I and II, set design, building, and lighting.

Suggested High School Subjects
English, social studies, mathematics including algebra, computer literacy, foreign language, elective courses in photography, speech, drama, and acting.

General Interest Areas
Theatre, acting, drama, film production.

Some Career Possibilities

camera operator	film director	stage manager
cartoonist	film inspector	technical writer
cinematographer	film producer	
college professor	photographer	
communications specialist	screenwriter	

Some Related Majors

advertising	dramatic arts	media study
art history/appreciation	fine arts	radio/TV
communications	liberal arts	

CIVIL ENGINEERING

Description
Civil engineering historically consisted of studies including the design and construction of dams, bridges, buildings, roads, and water supply systems. Today the scope of the civil engineer has widened to respond to the growing problems of a complex society including housing, pollution control, waste disposal, and the conservation of resources.

Plan of Study
The plan of study deals with physics, chemistry, calculus I and II, and selected engineering courses at the lower-division level. Later, more specialized engineering topics are emphasized, such as materials, structural mechanics, structural design, computer programming, and computer graphics. During the final semesters, supervised individual projects are completed; field work or internship experiences may be included.

Expect to Take
Concepts of engineering, applied mathematics I and II, systems engineering, statistics, foundation engineering, water resources engineering, electrical engineering.

Suggested High School Subjects
Social studies, advanced mathematics including calculus, advanced science including physics, foreign language, computer studies.

General Interest Areas
Mathematics, science, construction, professional engineering.

Some Career Possibilities

civil engineer	consultant	design engineer
lawyer	structural engineer	waterworks eng.
college professor	contractor	environ. eng.
materials engineer	systems engineer	

Some Related Majors

architecture	engineering	urban studies
ecology	soils/water management	environ. eng.
mining engineering	transportation	mechanical eng.

CLASSICS

Description
Classics is a general term that refers to the study of the language, literature, and philosophy of early Greek and Roman civilizations. Coursework in the major entails extensive reading of the early historians, essayists, and playwrights of both nations, very often in the original Latin, Greek, and/or other related ancient languages. A thorough grounding in the ancient history of the two civilizations is presented, with in-depth study of their earliest times, the period of their greatest contact, their conflict, and their ultimate collapse.

Plan of Study
Colleges offering a classics major vary considerably in programs, especially with respect to the intended goals. Some programs are intended to prepare for graduate study leading to the Ph.D. and college professorships or the pursuit of research; others expect the classics major to be combined with coursework in a modern language, modern literature, linguistics, or art history. Still others consider classics a program to be individually structured under close faculty advisement. These variations should caution the reader to compare programs carefully.

Expect to Take
Elementary and intermediate Latin, elementary and intermediate Greek, Greek and Latin poetry, Roman civilization, Greek civilization, Sanskrit, Greek comedy, Cicero, Horace, Virgil, women of Greece and Rome.

Suggested High School Subjects
Advanced English (AP preferred), advanced foreign language studies, advanced history, computer literacy.

General Interest Areas
History, languages, research, writing, teaching.

Some Career Possibilities

freelance writer	classics researcher	consultant
archaeologist	manager	social worker
art historian	college professor	translator
lawyer	museum curator	cultural anthro.

Some Related Majors

archaeology	linguistics	secondary ed.
history	philosophy	English literature
comparative literature	English	foreign languages

CLINICAL PSYCHOLOGY

Description
This is the study of the diagnosis and treatment of psychological disorders and mental illness. It is the largest of the various specialties within psychology. Practitioners conduct laboratory experiments and research projects on animals and human subjects, administer psychological and intelligence tests, interpret test results, and form diagnoses. They also employ various counseling techniques, one or more forms of psychotherapy and, usually in cooperation with medical doctors, drug-based therapies for healing.

Plan of Study
The undergraduate plan of study stresses a broad background in all aspects of psychology. At the upper-division level, specific studies of human development, personality abnormal psychology, and learning theory are pursued. Supervised individual research is required, as are internships in counseling or therapeutic environments. A graduate degree is advised for all practitioners.

Expect to Take
Biology I and II including lab, calculus, statistics I and II, experimental methods, child psychology, psychoses and neuroses, group dynamics, seminars in current topics, supervised research, counseling internships.

Suggested High School Subjects
Advanced science including biology and chemistry, advanced mathematics through pre-calculus, computer studies.

General Interest Areas
Counseling, therapy, research, mathematics, statistics, data analysis.

Some Career Possibilities
clergy	college professor	editor
private practitioner	social psychologist	lecturer
clinical psychologist	consultant	technical writer
psychotherapist	social worker	

Some Related Majors
clinical social work	industrial psychology	social psych.
developmental psychology	personnel management	sociology
educational psychology	psychology	
experimental psychology	psych for counseling	

CLINICAL SOCIAL WORK

Description
This major is the study of the techniques, skills, and processes that help people to develop themselves as individuals and overcome personal or social problems with others. The major prepares for a career in the helping professions, working with mildly or seriously disturbed persons of all ages. Treatment of mental disturbance, marital problems, sexual dysfunction, and alcohol/drug abuse represent the typical work agenda in this major.

Plan of Study
The plan of study at the undergraduate level is an intensive one. General psychology and social work electives supplement a general education core curriculum for the first two years; human behavior courses, abnormal psychology, and social work techniques are emphasized later, together with extensive supervised clinical experience in a treatment setting. The B.S. or B.S.W. (bachelor of social work) degree is the final outcome; the latter is usually the route to graduate study and professional licensure. So many colleges offer the social work program that students must examine offerings carefully to find the most satisfactory curriculum.

Expect to Take
Social welfare, general psychology I and II, sociology, social work policy, social work processes, organization of social work agencies, internships, supervised clinical experiences.

Suggested High School Subjects
Advanced mathematics, advanced science, computer literacy, foreign language, psychology or sociology elective.

General Interest Areas
Counseling, social service, psychology, therapy.

Some Career Possibilities
rehabilitation counselor	consultant	marriage counselor
clergy	substance abuse	psychologist
clinical social worker	counselor	Parole Officer
sex therapist	gerontologist	
caseworker	veterans counselor	

Some Related Majors
counseling psychology	behavioral sciences	educational psych.
anthropology	social sciences	sociology
social psychology	clinical psychology	psychology

COMMUNICATIONS, GENERAL

Description
"Communications" is a broad term that identifies the art of expressing through speech or in writing. Programs in this area also may be titled "Communication Arts," "Communications and Media," or "Communications Studies". This major provides a comprehensive background in writing and speaking techniques, familiarity with the workings of the mass media, and the skills for utilizing the media to deliver the intended message.

Plan of Study
The plan of study includes writing skills development, speech writing and delivery, inter-personal skills development, principles of advertising, public relations, broadcasting techniques, history of the media, and related offerings. Some colleges may have a communications major with one in speech communications, journalism communications, mass media, or broadcasting. This is a popular major, offered by a large number of colleges. Since program quality varies widely, careful comparison of program majors is strongly urged.

Expect to Take
Introduction to communications, mass communications, public speaking, radio and television production, communications theory, small group communication, introduction to psychology, social psychology.

Suggested High School Subjects
Advanced English including speech and journalism, advanced social studies, art electives, foreign language, computer studies.

General Interest Areas
English, speaking, writing, public relations, social science.

Some Career Possibilities
college professor	disk jockey	lawyer
management trainee	media specialist	radio/TV
communications center operator	editor journalist	announcer/news
marketing/advertising manager	news copywriter	secondary teacher

Some Related Majors
advertising	liberal arts	media study
American studies	library science	radio/TV
journalism	marketing	sociology

COMPARATIVE LITERATURE

Description
This is the study of the study of the international community of writing and of literary criticism. Its goals are to analyze world literature from early times to contemporary work, to appreciate its development over the centuries, and to make some contribution through original work or further study. A pure major in comparative literature is difficult to find at the undergraduate level. More likely, it is a minor concentration within a program of humanities or letters.

Plan of Study
The plan of study begins with a liberal arts core curriculum at the lower-division level, supplemented by electives that lead to the major. Since this major demands extensive reading of works often in original languages, the student will need fluency at least at the reading level and should begin foreign language study early in the college career. Advanced work at the upper-division level focuses on development of analytical and critical thinking skills, as readings are frequently selected thematically, and works from different cultures and historic periods are compared. Advanced seminars in current topics as well as independent study and research projects complete the study.

Expect to Take
Introductory, intermediate, and advanced foreign language, Renaissance literature, European literature; Russian literature, Japanese literature, short fiction studies, seminar, individual research.

Suggested High School Subjects
Advanced English (AP preferred), foreign language study, computer studies, advanced social studies including world history.

General Interest Areas
Foreign languages, literature, literary analysis, research, teaching.

Some Career Possibilities
archivist	historian	librarian
literary critic	proofreader	translator
college professor	language instructor	literary analyst
magazine editor	teacher	writer

Some Related Majors
foreign languages	dramatic arts	secondary ed.
classics	English	English literature
international relations	library science	fine arts

COMPUTER ENGINEERING

Description
Computer engineering is the study of computer systems design, with an emphasis upon the integration of hardware and software development, using the principles of engineering as the foundation. This rigorous program uses an interdisciplinary approach combining courses from electrical engineering and computer science in one curriculum. See other major titles, "Computer Science" and "Software Engineering," to compare the differences.

Plan of Study
Lower-division courses include calculus and differential equations, chemistry physics, computer programming, and computer methods. Upper-division courses move toward advanced electrical engineering topics, advanced computer language courses, senior project development, and internship/group project experiences. A surprising number of colleges and universities carry this major; program quality and emphasis may vary greatly, so the student is advised to examine catalogs and manuals carefully. Qualified curricula should be accredited by the Accreditation Board for Engineering and Technology (ABET).

Expect to Take
Introduction to engineering, calculus and advanced calculus, differential equations, mechanics, electricity, electric circuitry, physics, microprocessors, internship, group project experience.

Suggested High School Subjects
Advanced mathematics, advanced science, computer science, computer graphics, technology electives in electricity.

General Interest Areas
Mathematics, computers, technology.

Some Career Possibilities
college professor	electrical engineering	lawyer
computer consultant	technologist	robotics specialist
computer engineer	entrepreneur	systems analyst
computer scientist	high school teacher	

Some Related Majors
aerospace engineering	electrical engineering	operations res.
applied mathematics	engineering physics	software eng.
bioengineering	manufacturing	systems analysis
computer science	technology	

COMPUTER SCIENCE

Description
This is the study of the theoretical foundation for the development of computers and their applications. The major considers the mathematical base for computers, as well as flow programming, programming systems analysis, systems interface, software development and related fields. An advanced background in mathematics is required, and working closely with data is helpful. In general, the B.S. program prepares students for advanced studies and research; the B.A. prepares for employment directly after graduation

Plan of Study
The plan of study stresses mathematics skills development and coursework in statistics at the lower division. At the upper-division level, the major focuses on the topics mentioned in the description section above, as well as on computer graphics, special topics, independent study, internships, and cooperative-education opportunities.

Expect to Take
Algebra, calculus I and II, programming methods, data structure, software fabrication, operating systems, computer graphics.

Suggested High School Subjects
Advanced mathematics including calculus, foreign language, computer studies.

General Interest Areas
Mathematics, computer systems, mathematical analysis, systems design, programming.

Some Career Possibilities

actuary	research scientist	technical writer
lecturer	computer software	lawyer
college professor	engineer	
mathematician	systems analyst	
computer hardware engineer	consultant	

Some Related Majors

accounting	business statistics	economics
international business	operations research	systems analysis
business economics	computer engineering	insurance
mathematics	software engineering	

CRIMINOLOGY

Description
Criminology is the study of crime, criminals, and the criminal justice system. It analyzes the nature of crime, examines the forces or conditions that motivate people to commit criminal acts, and explores the systems that enforce laws or adjudicate criminal offenses. Interest in this specialized major, also titled "Criminal Justice," is of particular interest to people seeking to pursue a career in law, and law enforcement.

Plan of Study
The plan of study combines courses in the humanities with psychology, criminal law, investigative techniques, administration of criminal justice, the court system, the parole system, and penalties for violation. At the upper-division level, and particularly during the senior year, opportunities for externship or a practicum with a local law enforcement agency may be available.

Expect to Take
Law enforcement techniques, criminal justice system, abnormal psychology, the criminal act, human development, penology and corrections, juvenile delinquency, supervised practicum.

Suggested High School Subjects
Social studies, psychology, computer studies.

General Interest Areas
Law enforcement, corrections, parole administration.

Some Career Possibilities
security systems manager	probation officer	social worker
police officer	security officer	technical writer
corrections officer	military officer	F.B.I. agent
prison guard	parole officer	lawyer

Some Related Majors
behavioral sciences	pre-law	sociology
clinical social work	psychology	
political science	social psychology	

CYTOLOGY (CELL BIOLOGY)

Description
Cytology is the science of microscopic anatomy, physiology, and biochemistry of the cell. Cytology examines processes at cellular level. Sophisticated techniques of biochemistry, biophysics, , and laser beam technology are some of the tools the student uses in researching the world of the cell.

Plan of Study
Two separate plans of study, cell physiology or cell biology, are usually offered. Both require intensive coursework in biology, as well as a background in such specialized areas as virology, immunology, toxicology, genetics, and cell structure and function. Independent research in topics of current interest will take a significant portion of the student's junior and senior years.

Expect to Take
Zoology, calculus and advanced calculus, statistics, physics, botany, hematology, cell biology research, independent projects in cytology.

Suggested High School Subjects
Advanced science including biology, advanced mathematics including pre-calculus, computer science.

General Interest Areas
Science, research, microscopic analysis, statistics, experimentation.

Some Career Possibilities

bacteriologist	cell biologist	corp. researcher
laboratory technician	research scientist	technical writer
biologist	college professor	
parasitologist	technical editor	

Some Related Majors

embryology	biology	anatomy
histology	microbiology	bacteriology
human/animal physiology	biophysics	biochemistry

DANCE

Description
The major in dance is the study of the theory and practice of dance, its forms and choreography. Colleges offering a major in dance seek to prepare students to become professional dancers or to teach dance and dance routines and principles to others. Dance is a performing art. As such, admission to undergraduate study depends primarily upon a successful performance at scheduled auditions and only secondarily upon academic standing in high school. Students may earn either a B.F.A. or a B.A. degree. The former prepares students for advanced study or a professional career; the latter prepares students for employment in such fields as dance therapy, dance education, or dance administration. Where available, undergraduate students are encouraged to compete for selection to the college's repertory dance company.

Plan of Study
The plan of study stresses the practice of dance in all forms including ballet, jazz to modern, historical forms, ethnic dance, and dance of other lands; the curriculum also includes core requirements in liberal arts studies. Reports, research projects, independent study, and supervised experimentation may be kept to a minimum; participation in college showcases, talent nights, and other performances are emphasized.

Expect to Take
Movement technique, modern dance, elementary/intermediate ballet, improvisation, historical dance forms, dance production, dance repertory.

Suggested High School Subjects
Social studies, mathematics to algebra, computer literacy, science to biology.

General Interest Areas
Dance, show business, acting, singing.

Some Career Possibilities
director	professional dancer	dance therapist
choreographer	dance instructor	
fashion model	acrobat	
dance academy proprietor	stunt performer	

Some Related Majors
cinematography	elementary education	occu. therapy
communications	fine arts	physical therapy
dramatic arts	music	radio/TV

DENTAL HYGIENE

Description
Dental Hygiene is the study of the principles, procedures, and practices of keeping the gums, teeth, and mouth healthy. While two-year programs stress direct patient care under the supervision of a dentist, the bachelor's degree is generally intended to prepare students with certificates or associate degrees in dental hygiene for employment as educators, researchers, or administrators.

Plan of Study
As an upper-division specialty major following an associate degree or certificate program in dental hygiene, the plan of study includes topics in pharmacy, periodontal care, cariology, and current dental techniques. Courses in psychology, human resources administration, and sociology are supplemented by supervised practical experiences. Data processing for the health professional and psychological aspects of illness are also covered.

Expect to Take
Oral microbiology, public dental health, health statistics, dental pharmacotherapeutics, mathematics, human development, supervised practicum.

Suggested High School Subjects
Advanced mathematics, advanced science through chemistry, computer studies, social studies electives such as psychology and sociology.

General Interest Areas
Science, mathematics, patient care.

Some Career Possibilities

dental assistant	hospital administrator	nurse
dental hygienist	bacteriologist	oral surgeon
dental therapist	laboratory technician	pharmacologist
dentist	microbiologist	physician's assist.

Some Related Majors

anatomy	health sciences	medical tech.
bacteriology	hospital/health care	nursing
biology	administration	pre-dentistry

DEVELOPMENTAL PSYCHOLOGY

Description
Formerly known as "Child Psychology," this field has expanded to include development throughout the lifespan, and it examines human behavior as it changes from birth to old age. Personality development, intelligence, language development, and mental and physical functioning are a few of the interest areas within this major.

Plan of Study
The plan of study covers all aspects of psychology at the lower-division level. At the upper-division level, coursework includes child, adolescent, and adult development; methods of developmental research; personality theory; perception and learning; seminars in current topics, independent supervised research; and internships conducting "live" developmental studies.

Expect to Take
Introduction to psychology, learning and memory, perceptual development, cognitive development, practicum in social development, independent research.

Suggested High School Subjects
Advanced social studies, mathematics including algebra, computer studies, science including biology.

General Interest Areas
Research, human development, science.

Some Career Possibilities
clergy	psychometrist	developmental
clinical psychologist	consultant	psychologist
experimental psychologist	counselor	research scientist
college professor	publications	
freelance writer	editor	

Some Related Majors
behavioral sciences	experimental psychology	personnel man.
clinical psychology	therapist	psych. for couns.
clinical social work	neuroscience	social psych.

DRAMATIC ARTS

Description
Dramatic arts is the study of live theatre. Sometimes called "Theatre Arts," it is the major for those interested in acting, directing, theatrical stage design, lighting, and scenery construction. To concentrate in one of these areas means to have a background in all of them, well as a knowledge of the history and literature of the theatre.

Plan of Study
The plan of study may include a personal interview prior to acceptance and, for performance majors, an audition. While some portion of the study is devoted to traditional academic subjects, the essence of the program lies in learning and practicing those skills which may lead to a career in the theatre. Proficiency in a variety of theatre skills must be demonstrated through work on actual productions. Colleges with a strong drama program support a repertory company in which students produce and perform several plays per year.

Expect to Take
Principles of acting, speech for the actor, stage makeup, play production, play analysis, stage sound and properties, theatre laboratory, senior practicum.

Suggested High School Subjects
English, social studies, mathematics through algebra, computer literacy, foreign language, electives in speech, drama, psychology.

General Interest Areas
Public speaking, singing, dancing, acting.

Some Career Possibilities
actor	drama coach	drama teacher
playwright	prop manager	stunt performer
director	drama critic	technical writer
producer	stage manager	fashion model

Some Related Majors
cinematography	classics	comparative lit.
English	liberal arts	media study
English literature	communications	dance

EARTH SCIENCES, GENERAL

Description
Earth science is a general term for fields of study that examine all aspects of the earth and its place in the universe. The principal earth sciences are astronomy, geology, geochemistry, geophysics, meteorology, oceanography, and geography. Each of these is an autonomous study offered by many colleges and universities, and most are described in detail in this volume for the student interested in a particular specialty.

Plan of Study
The plan of study for this major is somewhat broadly defined. Some colleges title the program "Earth and Space Sciences"; others identify it as "Earth, Atmospheric and Planetary Sciences." Whatever the name, the plan of study includes courses in geology, meteorology, and, in some of the more rigorous programs, geochemistry, and geophysics. At the upper-division level, advanced coursework in the area of specialization is supplemented with field studies or independent lab research which is designed to sharpen the student's skills in exploring questions of current interest. Internships, advanced seminars, and individual projects also may be included in the program.

Expect to Take
Physics I and II including lab, chemistry I and II including lab, calculus I and II, research methods, geology I and II, astronomy, meteorology, geophysics, supervised independent research, internships.

Suggested High School Subjects
Advanced mathematics through calculus, advanced science through physics, computer studies, science electives; AP courses preferred.

General Interest Areas
Science, mathematics, independent research.

Some Career Possibilities
agronomist	college professor	oceanographer
astronomer	geographer	petrologist
chemist	geologist	
climatologist	meteorologist	

Some Related Majors
astronomy	geography	oceanography
environmental science	geophysics	petroleum eng.
geochemistry	mining engineering	

ECOLOGY

Description
Ecology is an in-depth investigation into the basic principles that govern the relationships among plants and animals within their physical and biological environments. It is an interdisciplinary field and draws on biology, chemistry, and mathematics to study, monitor, and theorize in the areas of water quality, wetlands, endangered plant and animal species and conservation. The structure and development of an overall environment is called an ecosystem and forms the most important focus of study.

Plan of Study
The plan of study begins with a core curriculum of sciences, with special attention to biology and chemistry. Later, advanced courses in biological topics and ecology are supplemented with field studies or ecological research. Externships at field sites also may be required, providing the student with hands-on experience necessary to the pursuit of this career.

Expect to Take
Cellular biology, organic chemistry, ecology, genetics, calculus, embryology, botany, research seminar, independent field research.

Suggested High School Subjects
Advanced science, advanced mathematics, computer studies, science electives.

General Interest Areas
Science, research, environmental studies.

Some Career Possibilities
ecologist	geochemist	microbiologist
embryologist	geologist	oceanographer
environmental scientist	lawyer	political scientist
geneticist	lobbyist	research scientist

Some Related Majors
animal sciences	environmental science	oceanography
earth sciences	geology	soils/water man.
environmental engineering	marine biology	genetics

ECONOMICS

Description Economics is concerned with the production, distribution, and exchange of goods and services. The effect of supply and demand on market and employment trends and the impact of these trends on governmental policies are integral parts of this major. Also included are the study of different types of economic systems in use around the world, topics in foreign exchange, and international trade.

Plan of Study
The plan of study includes basic economic topics such as economic theory, market theory, money and banking, economic statistics, comparative economic systems, and public finance. Field studies and internships in economic research may be available, as well as cooperative education programs that include working part-time for local employers. Seminar and independent study opportunities may be offered to exceptional students. Dual majors in economics and statistics, economics and mathematics, and economics and geography are also available.

Expect to Take
Introduction to economics, microeconomics, macroeconomics, public finance, labor economics or labor relations, international economics, wage theory, economic history, statistics I and II, selected topics in economics, modern economic problems.

Suggested High School Subjects
Advanced social studies, advanced mathematics, computer studies, economics electives.

General Interest Areas
Mathematics, statistics, research.

Some Career Possibilities
accountant/C.P.A.	bank manager	lawyer
actuary	credit analyst	statistician
appraiser	economist	stock broker
auditor	insurance broker	underwriter

Some Related Majors
accounting	business economics	history
applied mathematics	business statistics	international bus.
business administration	computer science	political science

EDUCATION OF THE DEAF

Description
This specialized major within the field of education prepares students to work with hearing-impaired children and adults. Hospitals, rehabilitation centers, and schools for the deaf are the usual settings for this work, with most time spent teaching signing, lip reading, and other communication skills. In addition, teachers of the deaf may be responsible for teaching life skills, such as cooking or personal hygiene, as well as academic subjects such as mathematics or social studies.

Plan of Study
The plan of study begins with a core curriculum of academic subjects, with electives in signing and introduction to audiology. At the upper-division level, coursework focuses on techniques for diagnosis, treatment, and remediation of clients. Experience working with actual clients is emphasized through extensive clinical practice under the supervision of a trained professional or faculty member.

Expect to Take
Anatomy and physiology, organization of speech and hearing programs, auditory rehabilitation, speech and hearing clinical methods, student teaching.

Suggested High School Subjects
Advanced science and mathematics, computer literacy, foreign language, speech/public speaking electives.

General Interest Areas
Rehabilitation, science, social service, education and training.

Some Career Possibilities
educator of the hearing-impaired	hospital administrator	social worker
college professor	psychologist	therapist
consultant	rehabilitation counselor	psychiatrist
	rehabilitation supervisor	

Some Related Majors
anatomy	educational psychology	nursing
behavioral sciences	linguistics	special education
clinical psychology	medical technology	speech path./aud.

EDUCATION OF THE GIFTED

Description
This major is the study of the psychology of gifted and talented children, teaching techniques and methods that will enhance such giftedness, and of strategies for identifying talented young people. Though most often a study at the graduate level, it may be coupled with another social science subject in a dual-major program for teacher certification.

Plan of Study
The plan of study features a core curriculum rich in social science subjects such as psychology and sociology. At the upper-division level, educational methods instructing talented students, educational assessment of giftedness, instructional techniques for communicating specific subjects, and selected electives such as developmental psychology are emphasized. Student teaching experiences with talented students are available and opportunities for individual research projects may be possible with advisement of a faculty member.

Expect to Take
Introduction to psychology, educational methods with gifted students, special education concepts, materials in gifted education, adolescent psychology, introduction to thinking, reading/mathematics instruction of gifted students.

Suggested High School Subjects
Advanced English, social studies, math, and science, computer studies, foreign language, social science electives.

General Interest Areas
Teaching, social service, research.

Some Career Possibilities
special education teacher	secondary school teacher	counselor
psychologist	clinical psychologist	developmental
research scientist	college instructor	psychologist

Some Related Majors
anthropology	liberal arts	sociology
behavioral sciences	pre-medicine	
clinical psychology	psychology	
developmental psychology	social psychology	

EDUCATIONAL PSYCHOLOGY

Description
This major is the branch of applied psychology that studies the problems and practices teaching and learning. Students of the field seek to discover practical applications for theoretical findings in the teaching/learning environment. Students conduct occasional experiments using various teaching strategies with the aim of finding the variables that make for effective teaching and more efficient learning. A small number of undergraduate colleges offer this as a true major area of study.

Plan of Study
The plan of study begins with a firm grounding in general psychology, college algebra, and statistics/probability. At the upper-division level, studies will concentrate on learning theory, cognitive development, perception, memory, teaching styles, experimental method, independent research, and internship experiences. The reader is cautioned to look carefully at those schools which claim this major. As a profession, it is more appropriately pursued at the graduate level.

Expect to Take
Introduction to psychology, statistics, mathematics, personality theory, theories of education, child psychology, cognitive processes, field work in educational psychology, seminars in specialized topics.

Suggested High School Subjects
Advanced social studies, mathematics including algebra, computer studies, science including biology.

General Interest Areas
Education, child development, mathematics, statistics, analysis of data.

Some Career Possibilities

college professor	educational therapist	research psych.
educational administrator	educational writer	social psych.
educational consultant	government psychologist	
educational psychologist	management consultant	

Some Related Majors

behavioral sciences	psychology	social psych.
developmental psychology	psychology for	sociology
experimental psychology	counseling	

ELECTRICAL ENGINEERING

Description
This major is the study of electricity and its application to technology and daily living. Electrical engineers today function in a broad range of areas that include computers, communications systems, and microcircuits, as well as environmental control, biomedical engineering, magnetics, and power generation. Electrical engineers also work in aerospace, automobile design, high technology, and education.

Plan of Study
The plan of study requires a firm grounding in basic engineering concepts, along with expertise in physics, chemistry, and mathematics through calculus. At the upper division level, subjects of interest include circuit theory, electricity and magnetism, systems analysis, and computer programming for engineers. The program usually culminates in a supervised design project.

Expect to Take
Physics I-III with lab, chemistry I and II with lab, circuit analysis, digital systems, linear systems, solid-state electronics, thermodynamics, materials science, field analysis.

Suggested High School Subjects
Social studies, advanced mathematics including calculus, advanced science including physics, foreign language, computer studies.

General Interest Areas
Mathematics, science, circuit design, electricity.

Some Career Possibilities
aerospace engineer	college professor	enviro. eng.
management consultant	pilot	technical writer
automotive engineer	electrical engineer	lawyer
military officer	research engineer	

Some Related Majors
aerospace engineering	environmental	industrial eng.
chemistry	engineering	mech, eng.
computer science	environmental science	physics

ELEMENTARY EDUCATION

Description
This major is the study of the skills needed to instruct children in a range of grades which may include pre-kindergarten through fifth or sixth grade. The major encompasses the psychology of youth development, as well as preparation to teach several academic disciplines and aspects of personal health, hygiene, and grooming. All programs contain a teaching certification component. Also known as "Early Childhood Education."

Plan of Study
The plan of study begins with a general education core curriculum, together with electives in developmental psychology, children's literature, and understanding childhood behavior. Upper-division coursework focuses on methods of teaching academic subjects, use of media in instruction, abnormal child development, diagnosis of child behavior, and student teaching experience under faculty supervision. Additional seminars in special topics, independent research projects, or directed study may be required.

Expect to Take
Fundamentals of education, statistics, language arts in childhood education, teaching in the elementary school, classroom management, behavioral disorders in children, seminars, projects.

Suggested High School Subjects
Advanced English and social studies, advanced mathematics and science, computer studies, foreign language, social science electives.

General Interest Areas
Teaching, social service, young children.

Some Career Possibilities
college professor	social worker	school admin.
school counselor	textbook representative	
elementary school teacher	psychologist	

Some Related Majors
behavioral sciences	nursing	secondary ed.
English	psychology	sociology
liberal arts	psychology for	special ed.
music	counseling	

EMBRYOLOGY

Description
Embryology is the study of the development of organisms. The entire period of development, from sex-cell (gamete) formation to the point when the organism's systems have been completed, is the object of inquiry.

Plan of Study
The plan of study concentrates first on biology and a complete understanding of biological development. The emphasis turns, at the upper-division level, to a particular focus on cellular biology, the structure and composition of cells, cell analysis and differentiation, molecular genetics, and recombinant DNA theory. Independent supervised research in embryology and other related topics is often required.

Expect to Take
Biology, chemistry, biochemistry, calculus I and II, physics, embryology, cell biology, microembryology, developmental biology.

Suggested High School Subjects
Advanced science including biology, advanced mathematics including pre-calculus, computer science.

General Interest Areas
Science, research, mathematics.

Some Career Possibilities

embryologist	consultant	marine biologist
bacteriologist	ecologist	paleontologist
biologist	government technician	research scientist
college professor	lecturer	technical writer

Some Related Majors

anatomy	biology	human/an. phys.
bacteriology	cytology	marine biology
biochemistry	histology	zoology

ENGINEERING, GENERAL

Description
The engineering major is usually organized in one of two ways: as an offering of a school, department, institute, or center for engineering; or as an "engineering and applied curriculum. Competition is generally keen in colleges offering either mode of organization. Colleges vary widely, however, in specific engineering programs that are true majors Most provide great flexibility in programming, so students can elect dual majors such as engineering/mathematics, engineering/physics, or engineering/computer sciences. The enormous range of choice among the available programs must caution the reader to examine college catalogs carefully and to seek personal advisement from the admissions office or directly from the engineering faculty.

Plan of Study
Each specialty is distinct, with a core curriculum in mathematics and engineering science during the freshman year, followed by full admission to an engineering specialty in the sophomore year, with courses in that area thereafter. In the "engineering and applied sciences" curriculum, students are exposed to a broad range of courses in the life sciences, the social sciences, mathematics, and electives.

Expect to Take
Selections vary with the particular major selected, but generally include calculus I and II, applied mathematics I and II, physics I and II (especially mechanics) with lab, introduction to computing, thermodynamics, chemistry I and II with lab, specialized courses within the field of choice, field study or cooperative education programs with employers.

Suggested High School Subjects
Advanced mathematics, advanced science, computer science.

General Interest Areas
Mathematics, physics, design, research.

Some Career Possibilities
aerospace engineer	electrical engineer	mechanical eng.
college professor	environmentalist	petrologist
consultant	industrial engineer	technical writer

Some Related Majors
aerospace engineering	environmental	ocean eng.
chemical engineering	engineering	nuclear eng.
civil engineering	mechanical engineering	
electrical engineering	metallurgical eng.	

ENGINEERING PHYSICS

Description
One of the more rigorous undergraduate majors, engineering physics combines com work in mathematics, physics, and engineering. Where this is offered as a true major, it is designed for students who are considering electrical engineering who wish to improve their understanding of the physics of electrical phenomena, or for physics majors who desire a wider range of applied courses in electronics and electrical measurements.

Plan of Study
The plan of study limits the major to students who specifically apply for it during their college sophomore year and who can establish eligibility through the courses completed during the first two years. Precise course requirements must be pursued with close faculty advisement, a qualifying grade point average must be maintained, and a faculty recommendation must be obtained.

Expect to Take
Engineering geometry, engineering statistics, multivariate calculus, partial differential equations, introduction to quantum theory, advanced computer applications, advanced calculus.

Suggested High School Subjects
Advanced mathematics (AP preferred), advanced science (AP physics preferred), computer studies.

General Interest Areas
Science, mathematics, engineering research.

Some Career Possibilities
aircraft designer	astrophysicist	electrical eng.
engineering physicist	physicist	test engineer
astronomer	college professor	electrical res.
mathematician	quality control engineer	

Some Related Majors
aerospace engineering	geophysics	physical chem.
analytical chemistry	mathematics	physics
engineering	mechanical engineering	

ENGLISH, GENERAL

Description
This major is the intensive study of the literary arts of the English-speaking peoples and world literatures translated into English. Two broad areas of concentration, reading and writing are encompassed in the study of English. The reading concentration concerns the contributors and contributions to the language from its beginnings to the present day. These especially emphasize British and American literature as well as translations of works from foreign sources into English. The writing focus includes development of the student's own abilities in areas such as writing poetry, prose, fiction, nonfiction, journalism, and technical writing.

Plan of Study
The plan of study includes courses in English and American literature, composition, grammar, poetry, prose, syntax, and special topics of current interest. Specialized writing projects, independent reading research, and the production of original work may be required.

Expect to Take
Freshman composition, advanced writing, creative writing, journalism, literary analysis, old English, seventeenth- through twentieth-century British literature, American literary survey.

Suggested High School Subjects
Advanced English (AP preferred), history, foreign language, computer literacy.

General Interest Areas
Literature, writing, reading, speaking, teaching, social science.

Some Career Possibilities

college professor	lawyer	playwright
editor	military officer	publisher
foreign service officer	museum curator	reporter
freelance writer	newscaster	teacher

Some Related Majors

advertising	comparative literature	secondary ed.
classics	English literature	foreign lang.
communications	journalism	history

ENGLISH LITERATURE

Description
The largest body of literature written in a modern language, English literature has developed over fifteen centuries from the Anglo-Saxon period to the present. As an undergraduate study, this major includes in-depth and broad-ranging exposure to literature from both British and American contributors. The major requires extensive reading of the greatest contributions, as well as a passing familiarity with the works of less well-known authors, including poets, essayists, playwrights, novelists, and historians.

Plan of Study
The plan of study begins with survey courses in topics such as medieval literature, nineteenth-century poets, or twentieth-century British plays. The students courses about individual authors, or specialized topics such as Beowulf Chaucer, Shakespeare, T.S. Eliot, Joyce, Keats, and Shelley. Finally, courses in contemporary literature, literary research, problems of modern literature, and independent study, complete the major.

Expect to Take
Survey of literature, medieval literature, seventeenth-century literature, modern drama history of literature, Milton, women in literature, seminar on problems in literature, research in literature.

Suggested High School Subjects
Advanced English (AP preferred), history, foreign language, computer literacy.

General Interest Areas
Literature, reading, writing, research.

Some Career Possibilities
actor	freelance writer	secondary teacher
college professor	lawyer	social worker
consultant	librarian	stage director
editor	researcher	

Some Related Majors
advertising	comparative literature	journalism
classics	foreign languages	secondary ed.
communications	history	English

ENTOMOLOGY

Description
Entomology is a branch of zoology concerned with the study of insects and other arthropods. While occasionally offered as an undergraduate major, it appears more appropriate as a topic of graduate study, with many areas of research inquiry involved. Beekeeping is one of the better-known specialties within entomology. Others include insect diseases, pest control, the relationship of the insect world with humans, classification of insects, and the effects of pesticides on insects.

Plan of Study
The plan of study emphasizes the scientific examination of insects and includes topics such as physiology of insects, anatomy, morphology, taxonomy of the insect world, pest management, virology, insect vectors, spiders, and mites. Experience in laboratory settings is an important element of this major.

Expect to Take
Introduction to entomology, statistical analysis, calculus, general ecology, forest and tree pathology, invertebrate zoology, forest and aquatic insects, wildlife ecology and management.

Suggested High School Subjects
Advanced science, advanced mathematics, computer studies.

General Interest Areas
Science, mathematics, research.

Some Career Possibilities
beekeeper	entomologist	parasitologist
biologist	laboratory technician	research scientist
college professor	museum curator	teacher
ecologist	paleontologist	zoologist

Some Related Majors
agronomy	microbiology	ecology
human/animal physiology	plant sciences	enviro. eng.
marine biology	biology	

ENVIRONMENTAL DESIGN

Description
This major is the study of the techniques of design, with close attention to factors that affect or impinge upon natural or human-made environments. It includes an examination of the human-made environment, from urban design to architectural design, through the organization of outdoor living spaces and planned landscape. Other areas of study include industrial design, farmland design, or site analysis, as well as the design of interior living spaces. Each of these topics may be offered as majors in their own right however they may also exist as concentrations within an environmental design program.

Plan of Study
The plan of study at the lower-division level is a general core curriculum with elective work in art-related topics such as drawing, principles of design, and history of design. At the upper-division level, work intensifies with the technical topics of design, drafting, construction, and the creative process, all culminating in individual supervised design projects. Internship experiences working with environmental design agencies or private consulting firms also may be available.

Expect to Take
Algebra, philosophy of art, techniques of design, materials and methods of design, architectural construction, problems in modern architecture, visual arts, art history, supervised design projects, internships.

Suggested High School Subjects
Advanced mathematics, advanced science, computer studies, art electives, architectural drawing, creative design.

General Interest Areas
Design, art, architecture, ecology, environment, health.

Some Career Possibilities

architect	construction engineer	enviro. scientist
college professor	consultant	freelance writer
commercial artist	draftsman	interior designer
construction designer	environmental designer	teacher

Some Related Majors

architecture	fine arts	urban studies
civil engineering	home economics	
ecology	interior design	
environmental engineering	landscape architecture	

ENVIRONMENTAL ENGINEERING

Description
This major is the study of technologies that conserve limited material and energy resources. There are two sides to this task: reducing environmental hazards and converting potential liabilities into energy-related assets. More than simply a pure engineering science, this major requires a broad understanding of ecology, the effects of pollutants on animals and human beings, and the application of engineering principles to elements that are endangering the environment.

Plan of Study
The plan of study includes a firm foundation in engineering concepts, physics, chemistry, and calculus. At the upper-division level, engineering courses are supplemented with studies in biology and ecology to provide the necessary background for a synthesis of the fields of engineering and environmental study. In the senior year, opportunities for internships or directed field experience may be available.

Expect to Take
Physics I–III with lab, chemistry with lab, calculus, systems dynamics, thermodynamics, introduction to design, fluid mechanics, biology with lab, ecology, environmental science.

Suggested High School Subjects
Social studies, advanced mathematics including calculus, advanced science including physics, computer studies, electives in ecology or related subjects.

General Interest Areas
Science, ecology, pollution study.

Some Career Possibilities
environmental engineer	environmental lawyer	pollution officer
college professor	lecturer	research scientist
consultant	pollution control	teacher
ecologist	engineer	technical writer

Some Related Majors
civil engineering	metallurgical	transportation
ecology	engineering	urban studies
electrical engineering	ocean engineering	
industrial engineering	petroleum engineering	

ENVIRONMENTAL SCIENCE

Description
This major explores the planet's systems of energy and materials and attempts to understand the effects of human-made systems of technology on the quality of life. In our age of chemical and energy use, it has been recognized that certain substances and conditions of our world must be monitored on a regular basis. Using this information, we may develop methods to control the use of technology for safety and effectiveness. Such topics as toxic chemicals and pollutants, radioactivity, and endangered species are of interest to this major.

Plan of Study
The curriculum must be quite broad, with an eye toward the experimental sciences such as chemistry, physics, biology, and geology. The emphasis is clearly on scientific methodology, since the goal of the environmental scientist is to find practical solutions. Current and future problems are examined in a hands-on manner whenever possible.

Expect to Take
Chemicals in the environment, resources and wastes, case studies in environmental science, measurements, hydrology, environmental planning,
case studies in environmental science.

Suggested High School Subjects
Advanced science including biology and chemistry, advanced mathematics, computer science.

General Interest Areas
Science, ecology, pollution study.

Some Career Possibilities
ecologist	chemical engineer	pollution control
environmental scientist	environmental activist	range manager
agricultural agent	government employee	soil scientist
animal scientist	microbiologist	toxicologist
biochemist	parasitologist	waste manage.

Some Related Majors
agronomy	geochemistry	soils/water man.
earth sciences	marine biology	toxicology
ecology	ocean engineering	
environmental engineering	oceanography	

EXPERIMENTAL PSYCHOLOGY

Description
This branch of psychology emphasizes active laboratory-based research methods. The task is to manipulate the conditions of an experiment and record their effects on a subject. This requires close statistical analysis, a direct control of the experimental setting, and change of the variables of the experiment, and systematic change of the variables of the experiment.

Plan of Study
The plan of study begins with an overall examination of psychological topics and the experimental method. This is succeeded at the upper-division level by conducting supervised projects in selected areas. Controlled lab experiences juxtaposed with field study/survey-based work, provide as well-balanced a view of experimental variety as possible.

Expect to Take
Introduction to experimental psychology, statistics and probability, algebra, psychological measurements, perception, practicum in experimental psychology, group research, independent research.

Suggested High School Subjects
Advanced social studies, advanced science including biology, advanced mathematics including algebra, computer studies.

General Interest Areas
Mathematics, science, experimentation, data collection and analysis.

Some Career Possibilities

industrial psychologist	clergy	editor
college professor	research psychologist	technical writer
military officer	counselor	exper. psych
consultant	social worker	therapist

Some Related Majors

anthropology	personnel management	psych for couns.
behavioral sciences	physiological	social psych.
clinical psychology	psychology	
industrial psychology	psychology	

FASHION MERCHANDISING

Description
Fashion merchandising is the study of the techniques for marketing and distributing clothing and accessories to wholesale and retail outlets. More often offered as a two-year associate degree program, it is available at a few four-year institutions and may lead to a bachelor of professional studies degree. As a four-year offering, the major sometimes requires coursework in fashion design, preparing students to create the fashions to be marketed. The field can be considered a highly competitive one, with many young people seeking this area as a glamorous career. Be cautioned, however, that it takes a highly motivated, creative, and aggressive individual to find success in this field.

Plan of Study
The plan of study includes core courses in fashion, both design and merchandising, business administration courses such as marketing, sales, and distribution, electives in communication arts and fine arts, selected liberal arts, math, and science.

Expect to Take
Fashion design I-IV, fashion layout, fashion model drawing, fashion merchandising, fashion writing, pattern making, internships.

Suggested High School Subjects
Advanced art including the completion of a standard portfolio, college-preparatory business electives, especially marketing and advertising, computer literacy.

General Interest Areas
Business, art, design, selling.

Some Career Possibilities
college professor	fashion designer	market researcher
product demonstrator	sales representative	technical writer
consultant	manager	
purchasing agent	small business owner	

Some Related Majors
accounting	international business	communications
interior design	business administration	media study
advertising	marketing	fine arts

FINE ARTS

Description
Fine arts is the study of the creation of artistic works. This major is intended for the student who seeks the experience of creation rather than mere appreciation. Fine arts concentrations include ceramics, drawing and painting, photography, and sculpture. In schools devoted exclusively to fine arts, such specialties as graphic illustration, industrial design, jewelry making, or architecture also may be found. Admission to this major is contingent upon the presentation of a portfolio of work of sufficient quality and diversity to demonstrate real talent and to measure up to the competition of peers.

Plan of Study
The plan of study begins with a core curriculum of general education courses and art electives. Basic techniques of drawing and design are emphasized at this level. Later, students enter an area of concentration and focus on studies such as use of color, advanced esthetics, perception, and specialty projects. The collection and evaluation of a portfolio is frequently a graduation requirement.

Expect to Take
Fundamentals of art, use of color, design techniques, advanced design techniques, two dimensional design, three dimensional design, perception, the figure, supervised individual projects, internships, art seminars, portfolio development.

Suggested High School Subjects
Advanced mathematics, advanced art in one or more areas of specialization with emphasis on portfolio preparation, computer art/computer graphics.

General Interest Areas
Art, drawing, illustration

Some Career Possibilities

art director	lithographer	glass designer
illustrator	costume designer	sculptor
cartoonist	painter	graphic designer
jeweler	display artist	teacher
commercial artist	photographer	

Some Related Majors

fashion merchandising	interior design	cinematography
archaeology	art history/appreciation	liberal arts
architecture	landscape architecture	enviro. design

FOREIGN LANGUAGES

Description
Foreign languages is a generic term for a study relating to the mastery of one or more languages other than English, or to the study of a culture through examining the literature of that culture in its vernacular. Nearly every college offering a baccalaureate program provides a major field in foreign language study. The most commonly offered languages include French, Spanish, Italian, and German; other languages may be offered as special major options, or as dual majors allied to one of the four mentioned above. Additional languages offered may include Japanese, Chinese, Russian, Arabic, Portuguese, and Hebrew.

Plan of Study
The plan of study emphasizes the spoken word, with intensive language labs, the literature of the language, from ancient times to the present, and the history and culture of the country and its people. Some may include study abroad or an independent study option. A careful review of college catalogs is mandatory for this major, colleges vary widely in the strength of their foreign language programs and students seeking careers that demand superior language ability must compare programs diligently.

Expect to Take
Introductory, intermediate, and advanced language courses with lab, history, literature, and culture of the subject country, seminars, study abroad.

Suggested High School Subjects
Advanced English, advanced social studies, advanced foreign language (more than one recommended), computer literacy.

General Interest Areas
Speaking, writing, translating, teaching, interpreting.

Some Career Possibilities
college professor	publications translator	secondary teacher
lecturer	international trade	lawyer
diplomat	specialist	text author/ed.
military officer	researcher	
foreign service officer	interpreter/translator	

Some Related Majors
anthropology	history	English
English literature	comparative literature	secondary ed.
classics	international relations	

FORESTRY

Description
Forestry is the art, science, and practice of managing forest and wildlife resources. Integral to this major are techniques to maintain forests and their wildlife, to analyze and evaluate lumber and wood requirements, and to protect watersheds and preserve recreational areas. Characteristics of tree growth, topography, drainage, and fire prevention are included. The federal government, all state governments, and a number of private-sector companies involved in the lumber industry employ forestry graduates.

Plan of Study
The plan of study is a rigorously scientific one. Coursework usually begins with biology, chemistry, calculus, and social science, later moving to more specialized areas such as botany, climatology, silviculture, forest pathology, soils, and geology. Schools offering forestry as a true major frequently provide dual-major opportunities, such as forestry/ biology, forestry/environmental studies, forestry/chemistry, or forestry/resources management. Close examination of catalogs and contact with admissions offices can clear up much confusion.

Expect to Take
Introduction to forestry, forest mensuration, soils, meteorology, range management, silviculture, soil conservation, resources policy and management, biology, chemistry.

Suggested High School Subjects
Science including biology and chemistry, mathematics including algebra, computer science.

General Interest Areas
Science, mathematics, conservation, ecology, wildlife.

Some Career Possibilities
ecologist	farmer	forest engineer
forest ranger	plant physiologist	wildlife manager
entomologist	fisheries manager	forest pathologist
forest supervisor	technical writer	zoologist

Some Related Majors
agronomy	environmental science	soils/water man.
botany	geology	
earth sciences	microbiology	
environmental engineering	plant sciences	

GENETICS

Description
Genetics is the study of the chemical nature of genes, the general principles governing their transmission, and the mode of action of genes at the chemical level. The emphasis is on an examination of the characteristics of inheritance, the role of chromosomes in genetic inheritance, and the analysis of methods to affect the process.

Plan of Study
The plan of study includes biology-oriented courses and a one or two year concentration in genetics. The students' time is devoted to such topics as cell biology, bacteriophages, protein secretion, kinetics and mechanics of viral growth, chemotaxis, and DNA theory, as well as supervised independent research in current topics in genetics.

Expect to Take
General biology with lab, biochemistry, calculus I and II, introduction to genetics, advanced genetics, virology, experimental methods, independent research.

Suggested High School Subjects
Advanced science including biology, advanced mathematics including pre-calculus, computer science.

General Interest Areas
Mathematics, science, research, experimentation, close analysis of data.

Some Career Possibilities

bacteriologist	embryologist	lab assistant
parasitologist	research scientist	technical writer
college instructor	geneticist	microbiologist
pathologist	technical editor	zoologist

Some Related Majors

anatomy	embryology	biochemistry
botany	bacteriology	zoology
animal sciences	histology	

GEOCHEMISTRY

Description
Geochemistry is the study of the relationship of chemistry and physics to the processes within the earth, such as the changing composition of rock, the growth and development of minerals, and the formation and movement of petroleum. Geochemists analyze ancient sedimentary rock through chemical means to study how the oceans and the atmosphere may have changed and how life may have begun. They are also concerned with the problems of environmental pollution.

Plan of Study
The plan of study includes a rigorous grounding in laboratory chemistry, physics, and calculus at the lower-division level. The upper-division level includes topics in introductory through advanced geochemistry with appropriate supplementary work in related sciences such as geology, petrology, and supervised independent research projects during the senior year. Field research experiences, internships, and externships also may be expected.

Expect to Take
Physics I and II with lab, general chemistry I and II with lab, calculus I and II, applied mathematics I and II, aqueous geochemistry, paleontology, geology with lab, petrology, analytical geophysics, independent research project, advanced geochemistry seminar.

Suggested High School Subjects
Advanced mathematics including calculus, advanced science including physics, computer studies, advanced science electives.

Some Career Possibilities
chemist	consultant	geologist
oceanographer	petrologist	research scientist
college professor	geochemist	geophysicist
paleontologist	physicist	technical writer

Some Related Majors
chemistry	mining engineering	soils/water man.
earth sciences	natural resources	
environmental science	management	
inorganic chemistry	petroleum engineering	

GEOGRAPHY

Description
Geography is the study of the topographical characteristics, climate variations, and geological significance of the land masses of the earth. It is a major that is currently enjoying a resurgence. Once viewed as a "dead end" study, today geography has relevance in several new areas, including oil exploration and environmental/pollution control.

Plan of Study
The plan of study is career-oriented. Coursework is available in urban and regional planning, cartography, transportation systems, and political geography. This major has expanded its focus to accommodate the needs of regional, state, and federal governments and private and public organizations that conduct global research. Colleges offering geography as a pure major often have dual major programs, such as geography-economics, geography-regional science, or geography/regional/urban planning. Catalog analysis and contact with the college department during the college search are important.

Expect to Take
Introduction to physical geography, meteorology, basic cartography, geography of a region (Europe, East Asia, Africa, etc.), transportation systems, urban models and policy.

Suggested High School Subjects
Advanced social studies, foreign language, mathematics, computer science.

General Interest Areas
Social sciences, politics, law, planning systems, computers.

Some Career Possibilities

cartographer	political geographer	geographer
physical geographer	economic geographer	systems analyst
city manager	political scientist	lawyer
planning engineer	economist	
college professor	sociologist	

Some Related Majors

anthropology	economics	history
international relations	linguistics	urban studies
area studies	foreign languages	
journalism	political science	

GEOLOGY

Description
Geology is the study of the processes by which the rock structures and the landscape of the earth have come into being. It also involves the examination of the present interior and exterior composition of the earth. By reconstructing the sequence of changes in the earth's structure geology brings about an understanding of the history of the world. Geology has many applications in industry, historical research, environmental careers, and military strategic planning. Modern technological developments within science provide the trained geologist with a wide range of career opportunities.

Plan of Study
The plan of study at the lower-division level includes extensive coursework in laboratory biology, chemistry, physics, introductory geography, and advanced mathematics, calculus in particular. Upper-division level coursework includes intermediate and advanced specialized courses in geology, meteorology, physical geology, mineralogy, petrology, stratigraphy. In the senior year, field experiences, supervised independent research, and internships may be options.

Expect to Take
Biology I and II with lab, chemistry I and II with lab, physics I and II with lab, calculus I and II, applied mathematics, field geology, structural geology, fossils and evolution, paleontology, introduction to geophysics, supervised independent research, geology seminar.

Suggested High School Subjects
Advanced science including physics, advanced mathematics including calculus, selected science electives, computer studies.

General Interest Areas
Science, research, earth structure, environment.

Some Career Possibilities

meteorologist	physicist	consultant
military officer	research scientist	environmentalist
oceanographer	astronomer	geologist
petrologist	college professor	geophysicist

Some Related Majors

archaeology	environmental science	metallurgical eng.
earth sciences	geochemistry	paleontology
ecology	geophysics	petroleum eng.

GEOPHYSICS

Description
Geophysics is the branch of the earth sciences that uses the principles and technologies of physics to study the earth. It is distinguished from the other earth sciences by the use of instruments to make direct or indirect measurements of parts of the earth, as opposed to the direct examination of materials and samples more typical of specialties such as geology. Related branches of geophysics include seismology, the study of earthquakes, hydrology, the study of groundwater, and aeronomy, the study of the upper atmosphere above 100 km.

Plan of Study
The plan of study begins with a solid foundation in chemistry, physics, and advanced mathematics at the lower-division level. Theoretical and applied study in seismology, earth dynamics, marine geophysics, and the earth's gravitational and magnetic fields occupy the upper-division years. Supervised independent research seminars in specialized topics of current interest and internship experiences complete the program. For those seeking graduate study in the field, the B.S. is the appropriate degree.

Expect to Take
Chemistry I and II with lab, physics I and II with lab, calculus I and II, applied mathematics, mineralogy, reflection seismology, solid earth geophysics, thermodynamics, sedimentation and sedimentary rocks, independent supervised project, advanced seminar, internships.

Suggested High School Subjects
Advanced science including physics, advanced mathematics including calculus, computer studies, selected science electives.

General Interest Areas
Science, research, mathematics.

Some Career Possibilities

geophysicist	teacher	geologist
petrologist	technical writer	gov. scientist
research scientist	astrophysicist	
seismologist	consultant	

Some Related Majors

earth sciences	mining engineering	physical chem.
geochemistry	paleontology	physics
geology	petroleum engineering	soils/water man.

HEALTH EDUCATION

Description
Health education is the study of those factors that maintain a sound body, that promote personal hygiene and grooming, that enhance interpersonal relations, and that contribute to the well-being of the community. Health education is a mandatory subject in most schools at both the elementary and secondary levels. Topics such as drug and alcohol abuse, first aid and safety, nutrition and weight control, and some aspects of sex education are among the most important in the health education curriculum.

Plan of Study
The plan of study begins with a core curriculum of academic subjects, supplemented by electives in the health or physical education department. Upper-division work then moves to individual courses in the topical areas mentioned in the description above, and in health care delivery, stress management, emergency medical services, and independent research courses. Seminars in current topics and student teaching follow. Certification in physical education, athletics, or health sciences education may be obtained in addition to that of health educator.

Expect to Take
Health behavior identification, standard first aid, cardiovascular health education, drug and alcohol education, nutrition and behavior, critical health issues, independent study.

Suggested High School Subjects
Advanced science and mathematics, social science issues, computer studies.

General Interest Areas
Education, physical fitness, social science/work.

Some Career Possibilities
biologist	elementary health	physician
chemist	educator	psychologist
college professor	healthcare administrator	sales manager
drug/alcohol counselor	nutritionist	secondary health

Some Related Majors
anatomy	health sciences	medical tech.
bacteriology	hospital/health care	physical ed.
dental hygiene	administration	sociology

HEALTH SCIENCES

Description
Health sciences is the study of those techniques and procedures that are used in assisting physicians and other health professionals to care for the sick, rehabilitate the injured, diagnose ailments, or conduct research in clinical labs. Concentrations include cardiopulmonary specialist, extracorporeal technology, nuclear medicine technology, and rehabilitation specialist. Admission is frequently based upon completion of specific lower division coursework, the quality of which is the basis for acceptance to upper-division study. Many health sciences programs lead to graduate study.

Plan of Study
The plan of study begins with a core curriculum of academic work and selected electives including psychology, anatomy, physiology, and advanced mathematics. Depending upon the health science concentration selected, a fixed program of courses is taken in the first two years and evaluated by a college committee. The final two years are devoted to advanced work in the specialty, with emphasis on supervised clinical experience, direct patient care, or involvement in independent supervised research during the senior year.

Expect to Take
Biology I and II with lab, chemistry I and II with lab, calculus I and II, advanced mathematics, anatomy, physiology, biochemistry, advanced courses in the health science concentration.

Suggested High School Subjects
Advanced mathematics including calculus, advanced science including physics, computer studies, advanced science electives.

General Interest Areas
Science, medicine, health, service professions.

Some Career Possibilities
health science technician	nurse	phys. assist
cardiopulmonary specialist	paramedic	rehab. specialist
clergy	pediatrician	teacher
management consultant	physical therapy aide	

Some Related Majors
biology	medical technology	pre-dentistry
dental hygiene	nursing	pre-medicine
hospital/health care	pharmacy	public health
administration	physical therapy	

HISTOLOGY

Description
Histology is the study of the tissues of living organisms. Analysis of tissue structures in microscopic dimensions is a necessary component of this study. The histologist compares the normal and abnormal development of tissues, investigates the growth potential of tissues after embryonic development, and examines the changes that occur in tissues under a variety of natural and experimental conditions.

Plan of Study
Few colleges offer histology as a true major at the undergraduate level. This specialized study begins with general coursework in biology and microbiology, then narrows to topics in histology. Emphasis is placed on supervised independent research on current topics; internships or externships for continued experimental study may be included.

Expect to Take
Biology, chemistry, and biochemistry labs, calculus I and II, cell biology, basic and advanced histology, independent research, experimental work in a field setting.

Suggested High School Subjects
Advanced science including biology, advanced mathematics including pre-calculus, computer science.

General Interest Areas
Science, mathematics, research, experimentation, statistics, close analysis of experimental data.

Some Career Possibilities

histologist	paleontologist	research scientist
bacteriologist	corporate researcher	writer/editor
microbiologist	parasitologist	
college professor	government researcher	

Some Related Majors

anatomy	biology	cytology
embryology	marine biology	
biochemistry	biophysics	
human/animal physiology	toxicology	

HISTORY

Description
History is the study of past events and personalities in human civilization. One of the goals of the study is to gain an active appreciation of the past in order to better understand present events and conditions. In studying history, the student develops the ability to think critically, to evaluate evidence objectively, and to express knowledge clearly and forcefully to others.

Plan of Study
The plan of study begins with a firm grounding in written English skills and courses in the humanities and the social sciences including not only history and government, but also psychology and/or sociology. At the upper-division level, students may specialize in the history of a particular area (e.g., America, Europe, or Asia), or in a period of history (e.g., the Greco-Roman era, the Middle Ages, the American Revolution, or sixteenth-century Japan). The reader is urged to examine catalogs carefully to identify either the college that has the specific program of interest or the college that offers the most options.

Expect to Take
Introductory courses in the social sciences, European history, historical analysis, Napoleon, medieval Europe, history of India, ancient China, the Middle East in history.

Suggested High School Subjects
English (particularly reading and writing skills), mathematics including algebra, science including biology, computer literacy, foreign language, social studies (AP preferred).

General Interest Areas
Law, research, anthropology.

Some Career Possibilities

college professor	historian	journalist
librarian	reporter	secondary teacher
editor	intelligence analyst	
political scientist	research historian	

Some Related Majors

Afro-American studies	area studies	classics
comparative literature	international relations	secondary ed.
American studies	art history/appreciation	
English literature	political science	

HOME ECONOMICS, GENERAL

Description
Home economics is the study of the well-being of the family unit, the care of the household, and the personal needs of the individuals within it. The major encompasses child rearing, dressing, house care, eating habits, proper nutrition, and personal hygiene, as well as the ethics and interactions of family life. While most colleges offer home economics as an autonomous major, it is interdisciplinary in its content, drawing from sociology, psychology, and health-related professions for much of its material.

Plan of Study
The plan of study involves a general education curriculum at the lower-division level; electives of the student's choice may lead to an area of specialization. Concentrations include child development, food and nutrition, consumer education, home furnishings and interior decoration, and family relations.

Expect to Take
Human development, psychology, behavioral science, biology, clothing construction, food preparation, nutrition, personal resource management, marriage and family living, conflict resolution, consumer studies.

Suggested High School Subjects
Mathematics, science, computer literacy, college-preparatory business electives, foreign language.

General Interest Areas
Foods, nutrition, home management, psychology, sociology.

Some Career Possibilities

home economist	food/drug inspector	psychologist
teacher	food tester	research dietician
cookbook writer	freelance writer	restaurant man.
counselor	hygienist	textile designer
dietician	nutritionist	

Some Related Majors

behavioral sciences	health sciences	public health
biology	medical technology	secondary ed.
elementary education	nursing	
environmental science	psychology	

HOME ECONOMICS EDUCATION

Description
This is the study, viewed from a teaching perspective, of the family as an interpersonal and economic unit and the qualities and characteristics it requires to survive and prosper. Topics include nutrition and food preparation, textiles and clothing construction, and home management. As noted in the companion description, "Home Economics, General", this is an interdisciplinary major. It prepares the student not only for teaching in elementary or secondary schools, but also for potential employment with home extension centers or social service agencies concerned with home and family management.

Plan of Study
The plan of study in the first two years may include a general education core with elective focus on social science courses such as psychology and sociology. Upper-division work includes these specialty areas: food and nutrition, clothing and decoration, and family management and hygiene. Method courses in education, supervised student teaching, and some independent project work complete the curriculum; program quality varies widely and may call for considerable investigation to find a strong choice.

Expect to Take
Nutrition education, consumer economics, foods of the world, gourmet cooking, issues in home economics education, parenting, child psychology and development, family planning, student teaching, advanced topical seminars.

Suggested High School Subjects
Advanced mathematics and science, foreign language, computer studies, selected college-preparatory "life skills" electives.

General Interest Areas
Education, food preparation, family management, social service.

Some Career Possibilities
college professor	elementary school	restaurant man.
home economist	teacher	gerontologist
dietician	psychologist	secondary teacher
nutritionist	extension specialist	health admin.

Some Related Majors
anthropology	behavioral sciences	home economics
hotel/restaurant management	marketing	sociology
bacteriology	chemistry	
interior design	public health	

HOSPITAL AND HEALTH CARE ADMINISTRATION

Description
This major is the study of the organization and management of health care systems. Sometimes it is considered a health profession; more realistically it is largely a mix of health science and business administration. The focus of the study is the understanding of those regulatory, technical, and fiscal considerations that make for the effective delivery of health care services. This major is appropriate for one who seeks a career in hospital administration, nursing home management, or operation of a large professional practice.

Plan of Study
The plan of study includes a general core curriculum with electives in health science and business; such electives may include introduction to business, accounting I and II, and business law. The coursework in the specialization during the junior and senior years may combine advanced work in hospital administration, understanding Medicare and other Government policies, and seminars in current topics, along with advanced accounting methods, financial analysis, and personnel management. Some programs may offer a dual major in health care administration and accounting, for example, to provide the student with more options for employment.

Expect to Take
Applied mathematics, introduction to business, accounting I and II, policy analysis, financial management, seminar in current health topics, senior projects, internships.

Suggested High School Subjects
Advanced mathematics, advanced science, computer studies, college-preparatory business electives such as accounting and business law.

General Interest Areas
Business, management, health care, medicine.

Some Career Possibilities

accountant	department director	nursing home
college professor	healthcare administrator	personnel man.
consultant	health-related facilities	teacher
comptroller	manager	technical writer

Some Related Majors

health sciences	pharmacy	pre-medicine
medical technology	physical therapy	public health
nursing	pre-dentistry	

HOTEL AND RESTAURANT MANAGEMENT

Description
A hotel is a complex system, serviced by personnel with a range of skills and trades. Managing such a complex entity has become a specialized study under the umbrella of business administration, with its own array of courses and disciplines. This major is the study of the information and skills needed to administer and direct such an organization, from a sole proprietorship to a large corporate operation. Colleges offering the baccalaureate in this program frequently draw their upper-division students from those who have pursued a similar program at a two-year college.

Plan of Study
The plan of study is a practical one. Coursework moves quickly from theoretical business core courses including business administration and accounting to those teaching front office operation, registration and billing procedures, supervision of housekeeping services, food and beverage management, cost control, and personnel policies. Students also complete one or more externships of at least a semester's length in local hospitality related facilities.

Expect to Take
Introductory psychology, occupational psychology, management, facilities maintenance, purchasing, law for innkeepers, club and inn management, travel and tourism.

Suggested High School Subjects
English, speech elective, mathematics including algebra, computer literacy, business electives.

General Interest Areas
Personnel, psychology, business, management, law.

Some Career Possibilities
caterer	registration clerk	health inspector
purchasing manager	foods supervisor	waiter/waitress
food and beverage inspector	restaurant manager	personnel man.

Some Related Majors
accounting	communications	bus marketing
advertising	economics	personnel man.
business administration	home economics	

HUMAN/ANIMAL PHYSIOLOGY

Description
This is the study of the systems and structures within human and animal organisms. Animal physiology is also known as "Comparative Physiology." The major physical structures of animals and humans are studied, analyzed, and dissected whenever possible. Relationships among the seven major physical systems of the higher primates are evaluated after undertaking a thorough examination of each of these systems. Cell composition, chemical properties of tissue, and system fragments are analyzed.

Plan of Study
The plan of study is strongly based in the biological sciences, with particular stress on physical structures, developmental systems, and comparison of properties, from the smallest cells to vertebrates and man. This major provides excellent background for professional study in fields such as medicine, veterinary studies, and zoology.

Expect to Take
Human anatomy, comparative anatomy, human physiology, microscopy, mathematics including calculus II, genetics, physics with lab.

Suggested High School Subjects
Advanced mathematics including calculus, advanced science including biology (AP preferred), computer studies.

General Interest Areas
Science, mathematics, medicine, research.

Some Career Possibilities

anatomist	college professor	laboratory tech.
parasitologist	technical writer	zoologist
biologist	embalmer	microbiologist
physiologist	veterinarian	

Some Related Majors

animal sciences	organic chemistry	cytology
marine biology	biology	zoology
bacteriology	toxicology	embryology

INDUSTRIAL ARTS EDUCATION

Description
Industrial arts, known in some states as Technology Education, is the study of the tools, processes, devices, and materials that comprise today's technological systems. As an education major, this field prepares students to teach industrial arts courses in public or private elementary and secondary schools, vocational/technical centers, or proprietary technical schools. The school-based industrial arts/technology teacher may teach courses across the full range of industrial arts specialties, including auto, wood, drawing, power, electricity, and metals, as well as technical drawing, architectural drafting, and computer aided technologies; the vocational/technical teacher, on the other hand, may specialize in one area and instruct that exclusively.

Plan of Study
The plan of study begins with a core curriculum that includes general chemistry and/or general physics. Introductory industrial arts courses in each of the areas cited in the **Description** above supplement lower-division work. In the upper division, advanced courses in woodworking, graphic design, electronics, and automotive technology will culminate in independent study projects and/or student teaching at the elementary or secondary levels.

Expect to Take
Metals technology, graphic arts, offset lithography, machine tools, microcomputer applications, problems in automotive and power mechanics, methods of teaching industrial arts, seminars, student teaching.

Suggested High School Subjects
Advanced science and mathematics, computer studies, health sciences/industrial arts electives.

General Interest Areas
Mechanics, education, social service, computer technology.

Some Career Possibilities
automotive mechanic	school administrator	structural drafter
sales	elementary school	materials eng.
manager	teacher	tools designer
college professor	secondary school teacher	metallurgist

Some Related Majors
applied mathematics	mechanical engineering	computer science
labor/industrial relations	civil engineering	systems analysis
architecture	naval architecture	engineering

INDUSTRIAL ENGINEERING

Description
This major, also titled "Manufacturing Engineering," entails the study of the organization and conduct of manufacturing operations. The industrial engineer designs manufacturing systems and attempts to predict, control, and evaluate the results obtained from such systems. The industrial engineer has historically performed tasks that include time and motion studies, production planning, quality control, job descriptions, and job evaluations. Today, this person still carries on many of these tasks, especially in large plants and complex work organizations.

Plan of Study
The plan of study for this major is often considered to be interdisciplinary. After a background in physics, chemistry, calculus, and engineering topics in the lower division, focus in the upper division is given to a mix of topics in both engineering and psychology. Elective courses in areas such as anthropology, psychological tests and measurements, and statistics and probability are included. Internships or field/practicum experiences often are available.

Expect to Take
Introduction to engineering, calculus I and II, university physics, general psychology, statistics for engineers, manufacturing processes, production planning.

Suggested High School Subjects
Social studies, advanced mathematics including calculus, advanced science including physics, foreign language, computer studies.

General Interest Areas
Mathematics, engineering, planning, human resources, equal opportunity counseling.

Some Career Possibilities
college professor	industrial psychologist	sales rep.
heat-transfer technician	lawyer	technical writer
industrial consultant	plant engineer	
industrial engineer	reliability engineer	

Some Related Majors
chemical engineering	environmental	physics
civil engineering	engineering	psychology
electrical engineering	mechanical engineering	transportation
engineering physics	ocean engineering	

INDUSTRIAL PSYCHOLOGY

Description
Also known as "Organizational Psychology," this major studies the behavior of people in work settings. Observation of the effects of changing work conditions on productivity and job satisfaction, factors affecting personnel selection, on-the-job training programs, and improvement of employee morale are all facets of this program.

Plan of Study
The plan of study begins with a foundation in general psychology, behavioral sciences, and mathematics. Some colleges require an economics course and a computer science course as integral parts of the program; specific upper-division preparation includes courses in perception and interpersonal relations as well as work experiences and internships.

Expect to Take
Introduction to perception, motivation, group processes, statistics and probability, laboratory in human learning, special topics in psychology (seminar), field experience in an organizational setting, internship.

Suggested High School Subjects
Advanced social studies, science including biology, mathematics including algebra, computer studies.

General Interest Areas
Experimentation, mathematics, sciences

Some Career Possibilities
alcohol and drug abuse counselor	employee assistance coordinator	publications ed. industrial psych.
industrial therapist	personnel specialist	technical writer
	employment counselor	

Some Related Majors
behavioral sciences	developmental psychology	sociology
labor/industrial relations	social psychology	exp. psych.
clinical psychology	educational psychology	
psychology		

INORGANIC CHEMISTRY

Description
This major is the study of the chemical composition of elements and compounds that do not contain carbon. These include metals, radioactive elements, and the commercial acids widely found in the chemical industry. The knowledge of inorganic chemistry is central to the glass, ceramic, cement, fertilizer, and metal industries. The inorganic chemist seeks to invent new products, find new uses for well-known elements, and adapt elements and compounds to new technologies.

Plan of Study
The plan of study is developed under the close advisement of a faculty member. Lower-division study is dedicated to prerequisite work in physics, chemistry, mathematics, and computer studies, with selected electives in organic chemistry. Upper-division work focuses on intermediate and advanced courses with extensive supervised independent research in the senior year. It is recommended that students planning graduate study have a reading knowledge of a language other than English, such as German, French, or Russian.

Expect to Take
Physics I and II with lab, general chemistry I and II with lab, inorganic chemistry I-III, calculus I-III, statistical mechanics, structural inorganic chemistry, molecular structure and crystallography, supervised independent research, senior seminar.

Suggested High School Subjects
Advanced mathematics through calculus, advanced science including physics, computer studies, German, French, Russian.

General Interest Areas
Science, research, mathematics.

Some Career Possibilities

ceramic engineer	general chemist	mining engineer
chemical engineer	inorganic chemist	research chemist
chemicals sales representative	laboratory technician	teacher
college professor	metallurgist	technical writer

Some Related Majors

agronomy	ecology	organic chemistry
biophysics	forestry	physical chemistry
earth sciences	geochemistry	soils/water man.

INSURANCE

Description
Insurance is an orderly way of providing for financial risk and uncertainty. The potential losses that can result from accidents, fires, so-called acts of God, and other disasters can be minimized through knowledge of proper levels and types of insurance coverage. The few colleges that offer a true undergraduate program in insurance provide a very comprehensive foundation in the practical aspects of this subject. Degrees offered may be either bachelor of arts in insurance management or bachelor of science in actuarial science.

Plan of Study
The plan of study begins with core courses in liberal arts, business administration, and insurance. Insurance areas that receive in-depth coverage include casualty, life and health, property, liability, commercial multiple lines, financial planning, and pension plan development.

Expect to Take
Accounting I and II, business law I and II, principles of finance, principles of management, marketing, insurance contracts, research in insurance problems, administration of insurance.

Suggested High School Subjects
Mathematics including algebra, computer studies, selected college-preparatory business electives.

General Interest Areas
Mathematics, social sciences, sales, statistics.

Some Career Possibilities
account executive	actuary	claims examiner
insurance broker	lawyer	real estate broker
accountant	business manager	financial analyst
insurance underwriter	loan officer	stockbroker

Some Related Majors
accounting	economics	business stat.
computer science	business administration	marketing
banking/finance	international business	

INTERIOR DESIGN

Description
The growing awareness of the effects of the design of indoor spaces on human productivity, morale, buying habits, and other factors has fostered the increase in popularity of this study as an undergraduate major. Office spaces, waiting rooms, conference halls, and nearly any indoor area where people gather receive the attention of the designer. The emphasis of this major is on the optimal functional use of space rather than the superficial decoration of existing spaces.

Plan of Study
Often incorporated as a specialty within the fine arts department, interior design's plan of study stresses the design function in both two- and three-dimensional forms, as well as technical drawing, modeling of interior spaces, use of color to achieve mood or size effects, and related topics. Basic art I and II, art history, and other core art courses are integral. Finally, one or more semesters may be spent working in a designer's studio as part of an internship experience.

Expect to Take
Introduction to art, drawing I and II, technical drawing, interior design I–III, color in space, two-dimensional design, three-dimensional design, graphics workshop, art history.

Suggested High School Subjects
Art, history, foreign language, computer literacy, especially art/graphics.

General Interest Areas
Art, design, fashion, construction modeling (forms and molds).

Some Career Possibilities
interior designer	technical illustrator	display manager
museum technician	college professor	industrial design
set designer	commercial designer	
small business owner	consultant	

Some Related Majors
home economics	fine arts	secondary ed.
architecture	industrial engineering	social psych.
art history/appreciation	landscape architecture	
fashion merchandising	real estate	

INTERNATIONAL BUSINESS

Description International business is an area of specialization under the broad umbrella of business administration. It consists of an intense analysis of overseas business operations, selection of investment opportunities and evaluation of resources to support the investment, as well as an examination of the social and cultural variables involved in conducting business abroad.

Plan of Study
The plan of study begins with core courses in business such as economics, statistics, advanced algebra, and management and organizational analysis. Specialty courses in international marketing, international finance, and international business environments follow. The study of at least one foreign language to the point of real fluency is a requirement. Colleges frequently offer a dual major in this area, coupling it with a major in finance, economics, statistics, or marketing.

Expect to Take
Introduction to psychology, computers and information systems, operations research, financial accounting, marketing strategy, international financial management, a foreign language.

Suggested High School Subjects
Advanced social studies, mathematics including algebra and calculus, computer studies, selected college-preparatory business electives.

General Interest Areas
Business, international trade, finance, social science, law.

Some Career Possibilities

account executive	college professor	lawyer
accountant	editor	purchasing
branch manager	financial analyst	sales rep.
business department head	import-export agent	

Some Related Majors

accounting	business administration	foreign lang.
area studies	business economics	international rel.
banking/finance	economics	marketing

INTERNATIONAL RELATIONS

Description
This is the study of the interactions of nations with one another and the use of political power and diplomacy to accomplish national goals. The study is an interdisciplinary one, examining legal systems, political structures, the effects of geography and population size, access to minerals and raw materials for production, and economic forces that affect the way nations behave toward one another.

Plan of Study
The plan of study offers students a choice of concentrations within the major. Colleges offering this study as a true major may include courses in comparative politics, international economics, international affairs, diplomacy, and diplomatic history. The study also may be offered as a minor in conjunction with such programs as area studies, economics, or political science. Close examination of catalogs is advised; personal contact with an admissions person or departmental chairperson is recommended.

Expect to Take
Introduction to comparative politics, international organization, international law, legal systems of East and West, European diplomacy, communism and the Western powers, natural resources, international politics, seminars on current topics, supervised research, study abroad.

Suggested High School Subjects
Advanced social studies, foreign language, political science, computer studies.

General Interest Areas
Politics, law, international studies, diplomacy, languages.

Some Career Possibilities
college professor	foreign service officer	intel analyst
international lawyer	military officer	political scientist
editor	freelance writer	
management consultant	political analyst	

Some Related Majors
African studies	international business	economics
history	area studies	political science
anthropology	journalism	foreign lang.

JOURNALISM

Description
Journalism is a specialty in the communications field concerned with printed and online media such as newspapers, magazines, and broadcast media such as television and radio. Many publications employing journalists use a combination of print and Internet format. Podcasting is a growing field for independent journalists. A superficially glamorous profession, it frequently involves extensive travel, high-pressure writing assignments, close deadlines, and uncertain career paths. Relatively few colleges offer a true major at the undergraduate level; those that do often are able to provide internship experiences working with local news publications to enhance the employability of students.

Plan of Study
The plan of study emphasizes writing ability, analytical capacity, research skills, the preparation of written copy in accepted professional formats, and the skills to apply technical competency to creative projects. In addition, courses may be required in other communications areas such as radio and television, public relations, or allied professions. This is a competitive career area and so should be evaluated carefully before investing time and tuition funds.

Expect to Take
Introduction to journalism, news writing and reporting, interviewing techniques, advanced composition, feature writing, public relations, mass media.

Suggested High School Subjects
Advanced English, English electives including expository writing, social studies including American history, foreign language, computer literacy.

General Interest Areas
Writing, speaking, public relations, social sciences, travel.

Some Career Possibilities
investigative reporter	news writer	announcer
lawyer	proofreader	reporter
lecturer	public relations	technical writer
news editor	manager	

Some Related Majors
American studies	English	radio/TV
communications	English literature	secondary ed.
comparative literature	library science	sociology

LABOR AND INDUSTRIAL RELATIONS

Description
This major concerns the establishment and maintenance of formal working relations between employers and employees. It encompasses hiring practices, terms and conditions of employment, negotiations, implementing government regulations, and the provision of employee assistance programs to combat alcoholism, drug abuse, or other factors that impede job performance. Very few colleges offer this program as a pure major. Most consider it an interdisciplinary study requiring work in areas including psychology, sociology, and political science. Such programs may be titled "Labor Studies," "Industry and Society," or "Labor and Industry." Internships with local labor unions may be available or mandatory as part of the major.

Plan of Study
The plan of study entails a core curriculum in sociology, labor law, history of unionism, and problems facing unions today. The balance deals with specialized subjects including collective bargaining, ethnicity in unions, and unions and the modern corporation.

Expect to Take
Introduction to labor relations, political economics I and II, principles of management, microeconomics, socialism, U.S. economic development, principles of negotiations, history of the labor movement, collective bargaining.

Suggested High School Subjects
Advanced social studies, mathematics including algebra, computer studies, selected college-preparatory business electives.

General Interest Areas
Law, politics, business, negotiating.

Some Career Possibilities
administrative assistant	job analyst	lobbyist
contract specialist	labor relations specialist	analyst
employment interviewer	labor representative	salary and wage
industrial relations director	lawyer	administrator

Some Related Majors
business administration	industrial psychology	secondary ed.
clinical social work	personnel management	social psych.
hotel/restaurant management	psychology	sociology

LANDSCAPE ARCHITECTURE

Description
This major is the study of the planning, design, and construction of the landscape features around homes, schools, public, and commercial buildings, as well as parks and recreation areas. Landscape architecture includes not only the aesthetic placement of flowers, plants, shrubs, and other vegetation, but may also entail determining the location of roads, paths, and parking areas, and caring for the environmental impact of such construction.

Plan of Study
The plan of study includes courses in botany, plant ecology, architectural drafting, college algebra, and introduction to computer programming. Upper-division coursework is required in areas including landscape architecture, site research, site analysis, and landscape design studio. The undergraduate program usually leads to the bachelor of landscape architecture (B.LA.). In some colleges, the program is a five-year study which includes a mandatory off-campus work experience.

Expect to Take
Plant materials, city and regional planning, site grading, aerial photography interpretation, graphic communications, technical writing.

Suggested High School Subjects
Advanced art, mathematics including algebra, science including biology, computer studies.

General Interest Areas
Design, art, outdoor work, construction.

Some Career Possibilities

landscape architect	urban designer	enviro. policy
regional designer	civil service	preservation
small business owner	energy conservation	

Some Related Majors

agricultural business/economics	art history/appreciation	enviro. sci.
agronomy	botany	fine arts
architecture	environmental design	interior design

LIBERAL ARTS

Description
Liberal arts is a field of study intended to provide the student with a broad general educational background, rather than a specialized program or some form of vocational training. Liberal arts is very useful preparation for graduate or professional study in law, education, the sciences, or medicine. This is also an appropriate major for students who are "undecided" or want to use their undergraduate years to improve their academic skills.

Plan of Study
The plan of study at the lower-division level highlights a core of graduation requirements and selected electives from any department within the college. At the upper-division level, the student pursues a plan that results in the accumulation of 18 credits in each of three areas of specialization; this triplet constitutes the "liberal arts" designation on the college transcript. Internships, independent research, and/or field experiences may also be incorporated. Close advisement with a faculty member is encouraged. Guidance in course selection is key to a successful program.

Expect to Take
Prerequisite coursework for a B.A. degree and a program of course study in about three discrete areas of concentration.

Suggested High School Subjects
A college-preparatory academic program of study, including some foreign language study, computer studies, and electives.

General Interest Areas
College study, graduate/professional study.

Some Career Possibilities

accountant	physician	freelance writer
lawyer	entertainer	teacher
clergy	pilot	gov. worker
military officer	entrepreneur	
college professor	sales representative	

Some Related Majors

international relations	classics	psychology
anthropology	pre-medicine	pre-law
area studies	English	
philosophy	health sciences	

LIBRARY SCIENCE/INFORMATION SCIENCE

Description
Library science is the skill of organizing libraries and other repositories of information so their contents may be fully utilized. Whether small one-person sites or large, fully staffed urban, university, or specialized libraries, they are universally organized according to one of three prevailing systems. In addition, the use of computers for record-keeping and accounting purposes has risen sharply over the past decade; computer studies is an imperative skill for any aspiring librarian.

Plan of Study
Few colleges offer library science as an undergraduate major. The plan of study consists of a liberal arts core, including psychology, history, mathematics, and science at the upper-division level; the major study involves in-depth study of each of the three organizational systems, as well as library management, public relations, purchasing, finance and budgeting, personnel management, and special library services. Occasionally, an undergraduate program will provide a dual major opportunity such as teacher certification to prepare students for the position of school librarian. Library science is more easily pursued as a graduate study leading to the master of library science (M.L.S.) degree. A prudent evaluation and comparison of available programs is highly encouraged.

Expect to Take
Psychology I and II, library organization and management, book and periodical cataloguing, storytelling, specialized libraries, seminars incurrent topics, independent supervised research.

Suggested High School Subjects
Advanced English and social studies, mathematics, foreign language, computer studies.

General Interest Areas
Books and reading, social sciences, mathematics, science, languages.

Some Career Possibilities
archivist	college professor	school librarian
acquisition librarian	public librarian	media specialist
museum curator	editorial researcher	technical writer
bibliographer	research analyst	
proofreader	information scientist	

Some Related Majors
art history/appreciation	liberal arts	comp. lit.
English literature	communications	English
classics	linguistics	secondary ed.

LINGUISTICS

Description
Linguistics is the systematic study of language from the point of view of syntax and morphology and the development of language over time. More than the study of the acquisition of language, linguistics analyzes structure, sound patterns, emergence of language, evolution of language, and the effects of a linguistic system upon culture. Usually pursued as a graduate study, it is sometimes offered as a dual major with psychology, anthropology, speech, or specific foreign languages. Other undergraduate programs couple linguistics with teaching certification in English as a Second Language.

Plan of Study
The plan of study consists of coursework in areas including syntax, semantics, analysis of particular language groupings such as Romance languages or Asian languages, and the historical development of one or more of these groups. It culminates in field studies and independent research.

Expect to Take
Language and linguistics, introduction to phonology, comparative linguistics, language and culture, applied linguistics, sign language.

Suggested High School Subjects
Advanced English, advanced social studies, mathematics including algebra, computer studies, foreign language.

General Interest Areas
Language study, research, analysis of data, science, close attention to detail.

Some Career Possibilities
archivist	cryptanalyst	editor
librarian	philologist	research scientist
college professor	document examiner	lawyer
linguistics specialist	radio/TV announcer	technical writer

Some Related Majors
anthropology	foreign languages	comparative lit
English literature	communications	speech path/aud
classics	philosophy	English

MANUFACTURING/INDUSTRIAL TECHNOLOGY

Description
Closely related to similar fields of engineering, this major is intended to prepare individuals for practical careers in the research, development, and actual fabrication of materials, equipment, and other new products. The technologist will often assist a supervising engineer in product design, and may act as a go-between with a manufacturer during production. The major may also touch upon elements of industrial organization and planning, as well as that of productivity improvement. This study occasionally is found as a concentration within a general engineering program, and may be called "Manufacturing Engineering Technology" at some universities.

Plan of Study
The plan of study usually begins with a strong liberal arts base, including the preliminary mathematics and science coursework prerequisite to technology courses. There is an increasing emphasis on the use of computers in solving industrial problems; this will surely be an important component. In addition, at the upper-division level the program will lead students to integrate their knowledge and skills in order to solve industrial problems. Some business courses may also be required to enhance knowledge of management, statistics, and even accounting procedures.

Expect to Take
Calculus I and II, chemistry I and II, physics I and II, materials and processes, hydraulics, metallurgy, computer-aided design.

Suggested High School Subjects
Advanced mathematics, advanced science, computer science, accounting.

General Interest Areas
Science, business, technology.

Some Career Possibilities
engineering technologist	factory supervisor	industrial des.
manufacturing engineer	sales representative	technical writer
entrepreneur	industrial consultant	
research technologist	science teacher	

Some Related Majors
business administration	mechanical engineering	industrial eng.
industrial psychology	industrial arts education	op. research
engineering, general	mining engineering	

MARINE BIOLOGY

Description
Marine biology is the science that investigates the plants and animals of the saltwater environment; it is also known as "Marine Ecology," "Marine Science," and "Biological Oceanography". The major examines the aquatic plant and animal life found in bays, harbors, wetlands, and other ocean and coastal areas. The taxonomy of marine plant and animal groups and their relationships with each other and their environment are also areas of interest.

Plan of Study
The plan of study demands a strong background in the biological sciences and mathematics at the lower-division level. Work within the major maintains an emphasis on marine sciences, with ample time given to field work and laboratory experiences that will assist in current research in ecology or the environment.

Expect to Take
Developmental biology, biochemistry, organic chemistry I and II, marine ecology, comparative physiology, marine operations and research. Extensive hands-on experience is expected.

Suggested High School Subjects
Advanced science, mathematics including algebra, computer science.

General Interest Areas
Science, mathematics, research, water-related environments, ecology.

Some Career Possibilities
laboratory technician	botanist	technical writer
anthropologist	microbiologist	ecologist
bacteriologist	college professor	embryologist
marine biologist	oceanographer	zoologist

Some Related Majors
bacteriology	oceanography	enviro. sci.
microbiology	biology	zoology
biochemistry	organic chemistry	genetics

MARKETING

Description
Marketing is the study of the production, sale, and distribution of goods or services. Beginning with the product idea, the market specialist seeks to determine the need for the product, the most attractive packaging, means of effective advertising, sales volume requirements, and distribution sources. Candidates in this highly competitive field should be resourceful, imaginative, aggressive, and well-motivated.

Plan of Study
The plan of study includes core courses covering all aspects of the business environment. Other topics of study include accounting, finance, management (with special emphasis on sales and promotion), consumer buying habits and motivators, sales techniques, and analysis of distribution.

Expect to Take
Introduction to business, microeconomics, business law, marketing, sales management, consumer habits, and co-op work experience.

Suggested High School Subjects
Mathematics including algebra, computer studies, economics.

General Interest Areas
Business, sales, law, mathematics.

Some Career Possibilities
management analyst
sales representative
market research analyst

survey worker
college professor
military officer

political consult.

Some Related Majors
advertising
computer science
business administration

economics
business economics
international business

communications
real estate

MATHEMATICS

Description
Mathematics is the study of numbers and numerical reasoning in the abstract. Mathematics may be either pure or applied. The former usually involves the study of mathematics from a theoretical standpoint; the latter is embodied in such concentrations as computer science or mathematics for science. Pure mathematics is the major for students planning to pursue graduate study; applied math is generally the major for a highly skilled student who is seeking a math-related career. Whichever way one chooses, mathematics is excellent preparation for a wide range of careers.

Plan of Study
The plan of study varies somewhat depending upon the area of mathematics concentration. At the lower-division level, a core curriculum with mathematics electives prevails. At the upper-division level, students concentrate on subjects including pure mathematics, actuarial science, computer science, and mathematics education. Advanced courses are supplemented by seminars on current topics, research projects, or internships during the senior year.

Expect to Take
Calculus I-III, applied mathematics, linear algebra, Boolean algebra, fundamentals of computing, programming, advanced programming languages, number and numeration, senior seminar, mathematics research, independent projects.

Suggested High School Subjects
Advanced mathematics (AP preferred), advanced science, computer studies.

General Interest Areas
Mathematics, research, computing.

Some Career Possibilities

Mathematician	computer engineer	nuclear engineer
actuary	computer scientist	programmer
astrophysicist	demographer	research scientist
college professor	engineer	statistician

Some Related Majors

accounting	business economics	economics
applied mathematics	business statistics	insurance
banking/finance	computer science	op. research

MECHANICAL ENGINEERING

Description
This major is the study of the application of engineering principles to mechanical problems. Mechanical engineers deal with a wide range of activities including research and development, invention, design, construction or operation, and even the sales of mechanical parts and products. The mechanical engineer's expertise extends from construction of simple and complex machinery to power generation, machines and tools for heavy industry, pollution and the environment, and consumer products.

Plan of Study
The plan of study, as in all engineering fields, demands solid competency in physics, chemistry, and mathematics through calculus. At the upper-division level, subjects include mechanics of solids and fluids, conversion of energy, feedback and control, analysis and design, air pollution, materials processing, and automated manufacturing. The senior year usually involves an actual design project under faculty supervision.

Expect to Take
Physics I–III with lab, chemistry with lab, calculus I and II, applied mathematics, materials science, engineering design, stress analysis, computer-aided design, robotics, computer graphics.

Suggested High School Subjects
Social studies, advanced mathematics including calculus, advanced science including physics, foreign language, computer studies.

General Interest Areas
Mathematics, science, construction, product design.

Some Career Possibilities
research engineer	college instructor	lawyer
design engineer	reliability engineer	technical writer
automotive engineer	consultant	mechanical eng.
military officer	salesperson	

Some Related Majors
naval architecture	chemistry	ocean eng.
aerospace engineering	nuclear engineering	electrical eng.
environmental engineering	civil engineering	physics

MEDIA STUDY

Description
The production of films, video, computer-generated images and other forms of recorded or live communication are included in this major. Also known as "communication media," this study may be offered within a communications department or applied arts area. The history, theory, and analysis of media forms are explored, as well as their cultural and social impact; the emphasis may also include actual media production for use in television, cinema, broadcasting, and advertising.

Plan of Study
The plan of study includes both theoretical and practical courses combining the purposes of media with knowledge of how to communicate a message to an audience. Hands-on experience in the production of various media forms and training in the use of equipment leading to the completion of actual projects requires a great deal of time, effort, and imagination on the part of the student.

Expect to Take
Beginning filmmaking, introduction to digital arts, documentary basics, urban media, cultural impact of media, electronic image analysis.

Suggested High School Subjects
Advanced English, creative writing electives, drama, art electives, computer studies.

General Interest Areas
Art, television, film, communication.

Some Career Possibilities

producer	film researcher	announcer
college instructor	media specialist	lawyer
manager	freelance writer	technical writer
film editor	newscaster	
media librarian	historian	

Some Related Majors

advertising	cinematography	communications
marketing	music	radio/TV
fine arts		

MEDICAL RECORDS ADMINISTRATION

Description
Also called "Health Records Administration," this is the study of the management and organization of health information gathering and retrieval systems in health care facilities. The best such programs are accredited by the Committee on Allied Health Education and Accreditation (CAHEA) of the American Medical Association. At the conclusion of the undergraduate program, a registration examination is given by the American Medical Record Association; obtaining this credential is frequently required of those seeking positions of responsibility within the allied health professions.

Plan of Study
The plan of study requires a substantial familiarity with lower-division biological sciences. Courses in anatomy, physiology, psychology, and mathematics are supplemented by electives in the major. Upper-division coursework consists of detailed examinations of specific topics in health record administration, hospital law, medical terminology, and computers in medical recording, as well as clinical or field experiences in a hospital setting and internships in hospitals.

Expect to Take
Biology I and II with lab, calculus, applied mathematics, statistics, medical terminology, quality assurance, health care delivery, health statistics, medical science, field experiences/internships.

Suggested High School Subjects
Advanced science, advanced mathematics, computer studies, selected college-preparatory business electives.

General Interest Areas
Medicine, science, record-keeping.

Some Career Possibilities
health record administrator	college instructor	health super.
health insurance representative	hospital controller	programmer
admitting clerk	data processor	teacher
health statistician	personnel administrator	

Some Related Majors
computer science	physical therapy	occ. therapy
personnel management	nursing	pre-medicine
medical technology	pre-dentistry	insurance

MEDICAL TECHNOLOGY

Description
Vital to all phases of medical practice, this major is the study of the practices and procedures involved in the procurement, examination, analysis and reporting of samples of liquid or solid material taken from human or animal bodies. Samples include blood, urine, or other fluids, as well as tissues from organs and bones. Analysis will usually be by chemical means and results reporting will originally be in written form to a physician or other medical professional. The technologist generally works in a laboratory setting and is supervised by a pathologist. With a bachelor's degree, the technologist can become a department supervisor.

Plan of Study
The plan of study relies on a firm lower-division background in biology, chemistry, and physics. The last two years will emphasize advanced work in these subjects and specialized courses in the practice of laboratory testing. The senior year dwells heavily on the practicum. Since hospital facilities can vary widely, the student is encouraged to investigate the settings affiliated with the particular college to find the most suitable one. It may also be important to look for schools recognized by the Committee on Allied Health Education and Accreditation (CAHEA) of the American Medical Association.

Expect to Take
Anatomy and physiology, medical microbiology, methods of chemical analysis, organic chemistry, immunology, biostatistics, laboratory techniques, practicum in laboratory techniques.

Suggested High School Subjects
Advanced science through physics, advanced mathematics through calculus, computer studies, science electives.

General Interest Areas
Science, medicine, patient care, research, laboratory investigation.

Some Career Possibilities
pathologist	medical examiner	histologist
tissue technologist	coroner	research sci.
laboratory technician	funeral director	immunologist
urologist	pharmacist	

Some Related Majors
analytical chemistry	human/animal phys.	criminology
genetics	cytology	organic chem.
biochemistry	nursing	embryology

METALLURGIC ENGINEERING

Description
This major is the study of the structure, composition, use, and treatment of metals. It includes the processing of ores and minerals, extracting and refining metals by chemical means, and the melting, alloying, and casting of metals. Colleges offering this area as a true major are more often to be found in the Midwest and western United States near those places where metal mining and production are found.

Plan of Study
The lower division emphasizes physics, chemistry, the engineering sciences, and calculus as a minimum foundation. Junior and senior years are taken with topics including structure of materials, ceramics, and polymers; thermodynamics; heat transfer and diffusion; metallurgical fuels; and crystal structure of metals. Internship experiences and supervised field research are integral parts of the major.

Expect to Take
Concepts of engineering, physical metallurgy, deformation of materials, transport and kinetics, process metallurgy, and ceramics and glasses.

Suggested High School Subjects
Social studies, advanced mathematics including calculus, advanced science including physics, foreign language, computer studies.

General Interest Areas
Mathematics, science, metals, mining, exploration, research, and data collection and analysis.

Some Career Possibilities
chemical engineer	consultant	geologist
machinist	mining engineer	sales rep.
college instructor	foundry manager	lawyer
metallurgical engineer	petroleum engineer	welding eng.

Some Related Majors
chemical engineering	environmental	physics
nuclear engineering	engineering	mining eng.
civil engineering	petroleum engineering	
oceanography	geology	

MICROBIOLOGY

Description
This major is the scientific study of microscopic organisms, especially viruses, bacteria, fungi, unicellular algae and protozoa. The use of tissue cultures is an important part of this field; they are analyzed using highly specialized techniques. The major leads to professional research in plant, animal, and human diseases. Subspecialties in the area include industrial, agricultural, medical, and clinical microbiology.

Plan of Study
The plan of study usually focuses on a concentration in general microbiology, biomedical sciences or genetic engineering. Each requires a thorough grounding in biology, chemistry, statistics, physics, and biochemistry. Concentrated study within the specialty occupies the greater part of upper-division work, and may include opportunities for supervised research, independent study, or clinical experience in a hospital or research facility.

Expect to Take
Medical microbiology, calculus I and II, recombinant DNA, cellular immunology, hematology, microbial physiology, botany.

Suggested High School Subjects
Advanced science including biology (AP preferred), computer studies, advanced mathematics.

General Interest Areas
Science, research, analytical methods, mathematics.

Some Career Possibilities
microbiologist	embryologist	hematologist
bacteriologist	research scientist	zoologist
lecturer	freelance writer	
college instructor	technical writer	

Some Related Majors
bacteriology	chemistry	biophysics
chemical engineering	biology	histology
biochemistry	embryology	cytology

MINING ENGINEERING

Description
This major is the study of the design and building of machines, devices, and structures used to take minerals from the earth. As a career specialty, it demands the understanding of the entire mining process from exploration and mineral separation to smelting and refining technology. As a baccalaureate study, quality training can be found at only a select number of colleges. Students should search for programs that are recognized by the Accreditation Board for Engineering and Technology (ABET) and that are located in mineral-rich areas of the country.

Plan of Study
The plan of study begins with a solid grounding in laboratory chemistry and physics and advanced mathematics. Electives in elementary mining courses are available. At the upper-division level, planning, design, and operation of mining facilities are studied. Coursework encompasses development and economics of mining projects, mining analysis, exploration techniques, and smelting technology. Field experiences in the senior year are an integral part of the study, which is the principal reason for careful selection of the mining engineering program.

Expect to Take
Underground mining systems, surveying, surface mining, health and safety in the mining industry, mine structures, mine investment analysis, smelting techniques, advances in refining technology.

Suggested High School Subjects
Advanced mathematics including calculus, advanced science including physics, computer studies, selected science electives.

General Interest Areas
Engineering, mineral analysis, geology, field research, mathematics.

Some Career Possibilities
chemical engineer	stress analyst	mining engineer
research scientist	metallurgist	technical writer
mechanical engineer	structural engineer	refinery manager

Some Related Majors
chemical engineering	petroleum engineering	mech. eng.
oceanography	geology	
ecology	soils/water management	

MUSIC

Description
Music is a multifaceted major area of study that incorporates technical knowledge of composition, performance, arranging, and production, as well as the esthetic appreciation of the history, development, variety, and potential of works of music. Some colleges offer music as part of a liberal arts degree program; this option usually requires the smallest number of music courses to complete, as compared with the more specialized, performance music majors available in music. A program in music may award a B.A. or B.M. depending on coursework.

Plan of Study
To specialize in music with more intensity, students may opt for one of the following programs of study: performance, which prepares the student with advanced individual instruction for professional participation in concert and symphony orchestras, commercial orchestras, large bands, and recording orchestras; theory and composition, which prepares one to write and arrange musical works; musicology, which focuses on the history, literature, and cultural background of music; and music business, which prepares the student for positions in the marketing and merchandising part of the music industry. Since musical programs vary widely, students should carefully analyze their career goals and match them to available choices. Performance majors generally require an audition for admission.

Expect to Take
Introduction to music, music styles and structures, harmony, theory of music, elementary and advanced auditory training, history of music, musical practice, individual instruction.

Suggested High School Subjects
English with good reading and writing skills, advanced social studies, computer literacy, foreign language, electives in music, theory, and performance.

General Interest Areas
Music, recordings, composition, performance, theatre.

Some Career Possibilities

arranger	college instructor	music director
music teacher	orchestra conductor	music producer
music products sales	music coach	technical writer
music composer	professional musician	vocalist

Some Related Majors

communications	dance	dramatic arts
elementary education	radio/TV	secondary ed.

NATIVE AMERICAN STUDIES

Description
This major sometimes is designed to inform the student about the heritage and contributions of Native Americans. The history of these people is long, rich, and varied; because of this, the study touches on nearly every field within the social sciences, including history, geography, anthropology, sociology, religion, and archaeology.

Plan of Study
The plan of study includes foundation coursework in the humanities, with electives in psychology, introduction to native American cultures, and Indian tribal organization. At the upper-division level, courses focus more intensely upon specific cultural groupings, such as the Aztecs, the Mayan civilization, and the North American Plains Indians; independent research projects on topics of current interest and field experience may be required.

Expect to Take
Native people of North America, ancient Mesoamerica, Native American culture and religion, introduction to linguistics, cultural anthropology, North American geography, Central American Indian culture, field experience.

Suggested High School Subjects
Advanced social studies, mathematics through algebra, science through biology, computer literacy, foreign language, anthropology elective (if available).

General Interest Areas
History, American Indian culture, anthropology.

Some Career Possibilities
anthropologist	archivist	clergy/counselor
government agent	lawyer	research scientist
archaeologist	book editor	college professor
historian	research librarian	social worker

Some Related Majors
American studies	history	area studies
foreign languages	archaeology	sociology
anthropology	social sciences	

NATURAL RESOURCES MANAGEMENT

Description
This is the study of techniques for the intelligent use and orderly replacement of earth's resources for the benefit of humanity. The term is a generic one that incorporates several areas of specialization, which may include renewable natural resources, fisheries science, wildlife ecology, range management, natural resources recreation, and watershed management. Colleges that offer any of these as a major must be evaluated carefully to determine how the programs fit the student's goals.

Plan of Study
The plan of study consists of the intensive study of science in the lower division with biology, chemistry, and physics, supplemented by advanced mathematics and a small number of electives in the major. Depending upon the concentration selected, upper-division study consists of intermediate and advanced courses in the area, field experiences of internships in the senior year, and, in some instances, supervised independent research. Nearly all concentrations in the major lead to a B.S. degree.

Expect to Take
Biology with lab, chemistry with lab, physics with lab, calculus I and II, applied mathematics or algebra, range management, ecology studies, conservation practices, field studies, senior seminar, independent project.

Suggested High School Subjects
Advanced science through physics, advanced mathematics through calculus, computer studies, electives related to the major.

General Interest Areas
Science, research, conservation, animal husbandry.

Some Career Possibilities
agricultural engineer	natural resources	consultant
farmer	manager	physicist
animal breeder	college professor	ecologist
forester biologist	orchardist	

Some Related Majors
earth sciences	environmental science	plant sciences
ecology	forestry landscape	soils/water man.
environmental engineering	agronomy	

NAVAL ARCHITECTURE

Description
As originally devised, naval architecture had to do with the design and construction of naval vessels. The study included hull design, propulsion systems, ship systems, compartmentation, buoyancy, and navigation systems. Today, while remaining a narrow specialty in some colleges, in others it has been expanded to be part of the field of ocean engineering.

Plan of Study
Where naval architecture is a complete major, the plan of study follows the engineering model. Physics, chemistry, calculus (to differential equations), and engineering concepts dominate the lower division; in the upper division, coursework includes ship design, stress engineering, dynamics, and propulsion design. Supervised research projects, internships, and directed study of current topics are required.

Expect to Take
Physics I-III, chemistry I and II with lab, calculus I and II, introduction to naval architecture, hydromechanics, fluid mechanics, marine materials, computer-aided hydrostatics, projects in naval architecture.

Suggested High School Subjects
Social studies, advanced mathematics through calculus, advanced science through physics, foreign language, computer studies, electives such as mechanical drawing and drafting.

General Interest Areas
Mathematics, science, art, naval design, naval history, drafting.

Some Career Possibilities
admiralty lawyer	commercial artist	marine biologist
military officer	ocean engineer	ship salesperson
architect	consultant	marine engineer
naval architect	scientific illustrator	illustrator

Some Related Majors
architecture	mechanical engineering	enviro. design
industrial engineering	electrical engineering	transportation
civil engineering	ocean engineering	

NEUROSCIENCE

Description
This major examines the neurological systems of human and animal organisms and the relationships of those systems with each other and with the central nervous system. Areas of specialization within this broad domain include neuroanatomy, neurophysiology, and neuroendocrinology. This is a very research-oriented major, usually leading to graduate study such as the M.S., Ph.D. or, in some colleges, to the M.D. degree.

Plan of Study
The plan of study focuses on the basic biological sciences in the lower division. In the upper division, courses study the major systems that interact with the central nervous system within the human/animal organism. Students ordinarily elect to specialize in one system and, during the senior year, conduct supervised research on the area of interest.

Expect to Take
Biology, chemistry, and physics with lab, calculus through differential equations, introduction to psychology, anatomy and physiology, neuron growth, neurotransmission, independent and supervised research.

Suggested High School Subjects
Advanced science through biology, advanced mathematics through pre-calculus, computer science.

General Interest Areas
Mathematics, science, research, experimentation, medicine.

Some Career Possibilities

anatomist	college instructor	lab technician
neuroscientist	research scientist	technical writer
biomedical engineer	geneticist	neurologist
physician	surgeon	veterinarian

Some Related Majors

anatomy	cytology	zoology
genetics	physiological	exp. psych.
biology	psychology	
human/animal physiology	embryology	

NUCLEAR ENGINEERING

Description
This major is the study of the use and control of energy and radiation released from nuclear fission reactions. It includes the study of the development, design, and construction of power reactors, nuclear fuel cycle facilities, and radioactive waste disposal facilities; research and development; fuel management; safety analysis; and operation and testing of facilities and equipment. Additional areas of application are radiation technology, plasma physics, and reactor engineering.

Plan of Study
Few undergraduate colleges offer a true major in nuclear engineering. Those that do frequently provide a choice between two programs: a four-year B.S. degree program or a five-year B.S./M.S. curriculum. Both entail core coursework in basic engineering for the first two years, specialty coursework in nuclear engineering topics for the following year or year-and-a-half, then directed field work or extended projects under faculty supervision for the remaining time. The five-year program ordinarily culminates in a master's thesis or project.

Expect to Take
Physics I-III, chemistry I and II, calculus through differential equations, thermodynamics, heat transfer, applied nuclear physics, reactor physics, nuclear power generation, computer modeling of physical systems.

Suggested High School Subjects
Advanced mathematics through calculus, advanced science through physics, foreign language, computer studies.

General Interest Areas
Mathematics, science, physics, nuclear science, research, data collection and analysis.

Some Career Possibilities
college instructor	nuclear engineer	reliability eng.
consultant	nuclear physicist	technical writer
government engineer	plant designer	
military officer	plant engineer	

Some Related Majors
aerospace engineering	electrical engineering	mech. eng.
chemical engineering	engineering physics	metal. eng.

NUCLEAR MEDICINE TECHNOLOGY

Description
This is the study of the use, research, and applications of nuclear (radioactive) materials in the diagnosis and treatment of diseases in humans. Technologists administer nuclear substances, called radiopharmaceuticals, to patients, then observe the responses as they flow through the tissues and organs. The major is a highly skilled, and growing specialty within the health sciences, requiring intensive preparation and a rigorous screening process. A national certification examination must be taken prior to actual employment or graduate study.

Plan of Study
The plan of study requires the completion of a series of courses in biology, chemistry, and physics, along with advanced college algebra and calculus. Courses in anatomy, physiology, and nuclear theory also are included during the first two years of undergraduate study. With the approval of a university screening committee, the student proceeds to intermediate and advanced coursework in the technology, together with intensive practicum experiences in hospitals or medical centers. The curriculum concludes with the National Certification Examination.

Expect to Take
Biology I and II with lab, chemistry I and II with lab, physics I and II with lab, anatomy, physiology, medical terminology, nuclear theory, nuclear medicine, radiation biology, clinical experiences, hospital practicum.

Suggested High School Subjects
Advanced science through physics, advanced mathematics through calculus, computer studies, science electives.

General Interest Areas
Science, nuclear technology, medicine.

Some Career Possibilities
laboratory technician	nuclear technologist	teacher
college instructor	oncology physician	technical writer
consultant	radiologist	
medical supervisor	research scientist	

Some Related Majors
anatomy	health sciences	physics
bacteriology	nuclear engineering	toxicology
earth sciences	organic chemistry	

NURSING

Description
Nursing is the study of the procedures for caring for the disabled and the sick, as well as the promotion of good health practices. Many two-year colleges and schools of nursing offer a course of study that leads to eligibility to take a licensing exam. The baccalaureate major is intended to prepare leaders in the field: nurses who are not only skilled technicians in the health sciences, but who also have developed extensive management skills. Specialties include obstetric, pediatric, gerontological, emergency room and operating room nursing, as well as nurse-midwife and physician's assistant concentrations.

Plan of Study
The lower-division plan of study involves a solid foundation in the sciences, especially biology, physics, chemistry, and advanced mathematics, and in social sciences such as psychology and sociology. A performance review by an admissions committee may be required prior to upper-division study. The final two years focus on specialty courses in nursing and selected topics in medicine and culminate in a practicum or clinical experience under close supervision.

Expect to Take
Biology I and II with lab, chemistry I and II, calculus I and II, psychology, introduction to nursing practice, family health care, acute/chronic health problems, nursing leadership, supervised practicum, nursing seminar.

Suggested High School Subjects
Advanced mathematics, advanced science through physics, computer studies, selected science electives.

General Interest Areas
Math, science, health care, social service.

Some Career Possibilities

clinic manager	freelance nurse	researcher
nurse supervisor	laboratory technician	school nurse
consultant dietician	nurse educator	technical writer
food/drug inspector	physician's assistant	

Some Related Majors

hospital/health care administration	pre-medicine	embryology
pharmacy	public health	histology
physical therapy	dental hygiene	
	bacteriology	

OCCUPATIONAL THERAPY

Description
This is the study of methods used to help people recover or replace the basic skills needed for daily living. The study is not limited to the rehabilitation of job skills—those that would lead to salaried employment—but extends to helping patients regain their social, physical, or psychological ability to live independent, effective lives. With psychiatric patients, this may include the control of behavior, the discovery of a job skill, and overcoming moodiness. With the severely handicapped, it may include developing the ability to care for themselves or learn a skill.

Plan of Study
The plan of study at the lower-division level emphasizes physical and social sciences such as psychology, sociology, biology, anthropology, physiology, and anatomy. The major study at the upper-division level includes neuroscience, biomechanics, kinesiology, treatment techniques, prosthetics, and orthotics.

Expect to Take
Gross anatomy, comparative anatomy, physiology, group process, methods of occupational therapy, mental health, research in occupational therapy, treatment technique.

Suggested High School Subjects
Mathematics including algebra, science including biology, computer studies.

General Interest Areas
Therapy, science, mathematics, direct patient care.

Some Career Possibilities

counselor	laboratory technician	occ. therapist
physical therapist	public health educator	rec. therapist
home attendant	nursing instructor	occ. therapy aid
prosthetist	rehabilitation therapist	

Some Related Majors

biology	hospital/health care	speech path/aud
physiological psychology	administration	physical therapy
clinical social work	public health	
psychology	nursing	

OCEAN ENGINEERING

Description
Ocean engineering is the study of the effective and efficient use of the oceans and oceanbound environments. It is an interdisciplinary study encompassing engineering, ecology, and architecture. Students are taught to recognize, analyze, and respond in creative and imaginative ways to problems dealing with the ocean environments. Concerns of the ocean engineer may include oil and gas exploration, mining the ocean's mineral resources, designing deep water ports, planning new uses for waterways, improving marine transportation, and protecting marine wildlife and coastal regions from oil and other pollution.

Plan of Study
The Plan of Study begins with a strong grounding in physics, chemistry, engineering sciences, and calculus. At the upper-division level, extensive coursework focuses on engineering design topics; this is supplemented with work in biology, ecology, ocean systems technology, and related areas. Supervised individual research may be required, as well as field research in current topics and internship/externships.

Expect to Take
Physics I-III, chemistry I and II with lab, biology with lab, engineering concepts, systems dynamics, fluid mechanics, marine hydrodynamics, ecological systems, ocean engineering design I and II.

Suggested High School Subjects
Social sciences, advanced mathematics including calculus, advanced science including physics, foreign language, computer studies, electives in ecology.

General Interest Areas
Mathematics, science, ocean biology, research, ecology, environmental protection.

Some Career Possibilities
ocean engineer	environmental lawyer	technical writer
marine biologist	reliability engineer	marine engineer
college professor	management consultant	
military officer ecologist	research scientist	

Some Related Majors
chemical engineering	civil engineering	physics
marine biology chemistry	naval architecture	enviro. eng.
mining engineering	ecology	

OCEANOGRAPHY

Description
This major is an area of science concerned with the sea and its inhabitants. It examines how the air, the earth beneath the sea, and the coastline interact with the sea. Involved in this investigation are the disciplines of physics, biology, chemistry, zoology, and geology, as well as advanced mathematics. The major is most often found as a program of graduate study for career preparation. On the undergraduate level it is seen largely as a preparation for graduate work.

Plan of Study
The plan of study is first a liberal mixture of all the basic sciences listed above. The actual applications of these sciences to the study of oceanography are then implemented, with an emphasis on research technique. Marine organisms, marine sediments, and ecological considerations are all topics of interest. As with most research-oriented majors, it is wise to seek out a program that offers either a formal internship or a senior research project. Most colleges offering this major will be located in coastal areas.

Expect to Take
Biology, marine geology, calculus, botany, chemistry, physics, ocean I, II and higher.

Suggested High School Subjects
Advanced science, advanced mathematics, computer studies, social studies including geography.

General Interest Areas
Science, mathematics.

Some Career Possibilities
oceanographer	chemist	military officer
geophysicist	college professor	naval architect
hydrologist	marine biologist	enviro. scientist
chemical engineer	ecologist	

Some Related Majors
earth sciences	naval architecture	geology
natural resources management	environmental science	soils/water man.
ecology	ocean engineering	marine biology

OPERATIONS RESEARCH

Description
Operations research is a mathematically based concentration within the business administration major. Its purpose is to solve business and related problems using a mathematical model. Students learn to construct a model of the system to be analyzed, including its structure and constraints; state the objectives to be realized; and utilize mathematical techniques to find the best way to accomplish the objective,

Plan of Study
The plan of study usually requires a core of liberal arts courses with some business electives during the first two years, then proceeds to heavily mathematics-based major study encompassing such subjects as mathematical modeling, game theory, decision theory, networking, graphics, and flow charting. Dual major programs in operations research and either economics or mathematics are available in some colleges; by taking appropriate accounting courses it may even be possible to obtain the C.P.A. credential at the close of this program. At some colleges, operations research is considered a field of applied mathematics, management, or engineering.

Expect to Take
Physics I–III, calculus I and II, applied statistics, probability, macroeconomics, linear models and demand forecasting, organizational behavior I and II, optimization techniques, queuing theory.

Suggested High School Subjects
Advanced mathematics including calculus, computer studies.

General Interest Areas
Mathematics, research analysis, problem-solving, computer modeling.

Some Career Possibilities

operations researcher	college professor	systems analyst
computer programmer	research/development	
organizational researcher	director	
industrial engineer	management analyst	

Some Related Majors

applied mathematics	marketing	business eco.
computer science	business administration	systems analysis
banking/finance	mathematics	business stat.

ORGANIC CHEMISTRY

Description
This is the study of the elements and compounds that contain carbon, including those substances that constitute living matter. A much larger field of study than inorganic chemistry (over one million organic compounds are known to exist), the major involves the study of proteins, fats, and carbohydrates; materials such as silk, petroleum, and cotton; and synthetic materials such as plastics, paints, and many drugs. In addition, the range of knowledge is constantly expanding, making this major an area of increasing interest and importance in nearly every aspect of human endeavor.

Plan of Study
The plan of study begins with a two-year core curriculum in sciences, math, and selected electives. Courses in biology, physics, and calculus supplement courses in introductory chemistry, chemistry of compounds, and organic chemistry lab. At the upper-division level, intermediate and advanced topics in chemistry are supplemented by seminars, supervised independent research, and free electives. The B.S. degree in chemistry should be an accredited program, indicating appropriate preparation for graduate study in chemistry; the B.A. usually provides a more general background intended as preparation for graduate study in fields such as law or teaching or for immediate employment.

Expect to Take
Biology I and II with lab, physics I and II with lab, calculus I and II, experimental chemistry lab, organic chemistry I and II, chemistry of elements and compounds, physical chemistry I and II, junior/senior seminar, independent research.

Suggested High School Subjects
Advanced science, advanced mathematics including calculus, computer studies, advanced science electives.

General Interest Areas
Science, mathematics, chemistry, research, analysis and experimentation.

Some Career Possibilities
laboratory technician	pharmacist	consultant
research scientist	college professor	physicist
organic chemist	physical chemist	pest controller
chemicals sales	physician	secondary teacher

Some Related Majors
analytical chemistry	biochemistry	chemical eng.
chemistry	ecology	inorganic chem.

PALEONTOLOGY

Description
This major studies the fossil evidence of plants and animals in a biological, geological, and historical context. The paleontologist interprets what these fossils may indicate about their ancient environment and the development of life on our planet. Comparisons are also made with living organisms. Investigations are conducted using field techniques for gathering fossils and applying laboratory procedures to examine and label them.

Plan of Study
The pure major in paleontology is rarely found as an undergraduate program, though it does exist in some colleges. It is more likely to occur as a concentration within a more general program of study in earth science, geology, or planetary science. In fact, coursework in geology is usually the prerequisite to the study of paleontology. The program also includes topics in morphology and the classification of fossils, as well as extensive laboratory experience in the preparation of fossils and microfossils.

Expect to Take
Introduction to paleontology, micropaleontology, physical geology, historical geology, sedimentary processes, stratigraphy.

Suggested High School Subjects
Advanced science, advanced mathematics, computer studies.

General Interest Areas
Geology, biology, earth sciences.

Some Career Possibilities
anthropologist	geochemist	geophysicist
paleontologist	petroleum engineer	zoologist
bacteriologist	geologist	microbiologist
parasitologist	soil scientist	

Some Related Majors
archaeology	ecology	geochemistry
geology	microbiology	anthropology
earth sciences	environmental science	
marine biology	zoology	

PERSONNEL MANAGEMENT

Description
This major is the study of the processes and procedures that deal with the control, distribution, payment, health, and welfare of employees in a business environment. It has to do with the hiring and firing of employees, the regulation of wages and salaries, the management of benefit programs and pensions and, sometimes, the negotiation of contracts within the collective bargaining process. This study is a field of concentration within the business administration department of a college.

Plan of Study
The plan of study begins with a core of business courses. More advanced courses in this major are generally of a practical kind, examining methods commonly used in business to study employee evaluation, for example, or legal considerations in hiring practices and the treatment of employees, or evaluating insurance programs to determine optimum benefits. Senior seminars and independent research courses focus on case histories and problem-solving techniques to develop the student's ability to make competent management decisions.

Expect to Take
Wage and salary administration, pension and benefit management, personnel administration, industrial relations, performance appraisal, equal employment opportunity, employment law.

Suggested High School Subjects
Mathematics including calculus, computer studies, advanced social studies, college-preparatory business electives including business law and accounting.

General Interest Areas
Business, mathematics, personnel, administration.

Some Career Possibilities

personnel manager	consultant	hospital admin.
personnel analyst	accountant	technical writer
entrepreneur	sales manager	lawyer
military officer	government manager	
college professor	school principal	

Some Related Majors

behavioral sciences	labor/industrial relations	psychology
hotel/restaurant management	hospital/health care	pre-law
business administration	administration	

PETROLEUM ENGINEERING

Description
A branch of mining engineering, this is the study of the processes of drilling, producing, processing, and transporting petroleum products from field to consumer. Petroleum engineers apply their skills to deep drilling on land, off-shore drilling, shallow-water drilling, and related skills. Many aspects of civil, chemical, and mechanical engineering have had an impact on today's petroleum engineering specialty.

Plan of Study
The plan of study encompasses, at the lower-division level, physics, organic and inorganic chemistry, and engineering topics. At the upper-division level, work in well-drilling, reservoir analysis, petroleum production, and the laws of oil and gas drilling complete the program. Some colleges may offer an externship experience for a semester, in addition to a supervised project.

Expect to Take
Introduction to engineering, geology I-III with lab, thermodynamics, mechanics of materials, fluid mechanics, electrical circuitry, petrophysics, statistics.

Suggested High School Subjects
Advanced mathematics including calculus, advanced science including physics, foreign language, computer studies, social studies.

General Interest Areas
Mathematics, science, exploration, field research, data analysis.

Some Career Possibilities

petroleum engineer	refinery manager	college prof.
drilling supervisor	geologist	reliability eng.
platform manager	chemical engineer	consultant
drilling technician	mining engineer	

Some Related Majors

chemistry	earth sciences	mining eng.
geophysics	metallurgical	geology
civil engineering	engineering	ocean eng.
mechanical engineering	geochemistry	

PHARMACY

Description
Pharmacy is the study of the preparation, packaging, distribution, and storage of drugs or other medical prescriptions. Understanding the effects of chemicals on living beings is at the heart of this discipline. This knowledge is used in medical research as well as in clinical medicine. This science has applications for diagnosis and prevention of illness as well as for relief from the symptoms of illness and the cure of disease.

Plan of Study
The plan of study for the undergraduate degree, often called "Pharmaceutical Sciences," is usually five years long. Lower-division study emphasizes basic science and electives in the major, together with supplementary study in physiology and sociology to prepare the student to work with patients in health care settings. Upper-division work, the final three years, is taken in the college of pharmacy and consists of specialized advanced work in topics of pharmacy. Admission to the college is usually based upon student performance on the Pharmacy College Admission Test (PCAT). When evaluating colleges of pharmacy for admission, be sure that the college is accredited by the American Council on Pharmaceutical Education.

Expect to Take
Chemistry I and II with lab, physics I and II with lab, advanced mathematics, antibiotics, pharmaceutics, medical chemistry, seminars, internships, supervised practicum.

Suggested High School Subjects
Advanced mathematics including calculus, advanced science, computer studies, selected science electives.

General Interest Areas
Medicine, health, chemistry, patient service, entrepreneurship.

Some Career Possibilities

pharmacist	chemist	lab. assist.
biochemist	physician	technical writer
chemical engineer	entrepreneur	pathologist
pharmacologist	research scientist	

Some Related Majors

analytical chemistry	organic chemistry	health sciences
medical technology	chemistry	toxicology
biochemistry	pre-medicine	inorganic chem.

PHILOSOPHY

Description
The study of philosophy entails the logical analysis of the principles underlying human conduct, thought, and knowledge, and the nature of the universe. These "large" issues are examined, first, in the light of what prior philosophers have construed to be the answers and, second, by analyzing what contemporary philosophical thinkers propose as their solutions. From this study comes an understanding of the complexity of philosophical issues, the importance of critical thinking in their solutions, and the range of issues that need close analysis.

Plan of Study
The plan of study involves courses such as psychology, history, and anthropology, specialized courses in epistemology, logic, and ethics, the history of some philosophers, and courses in contemporary issues such as nuclear war, abortion, apartheid, chemical warfare, and so-called white collar crime. The skills learned in the philosophy major are applicable to a vast range of career areas, including law, business, teaching, publishing, computer science, public service, medicine, and foreign service.

Expect to Take
Introduction to ethics, deductive and/or symbolic logic, philosophy of language, political philosophy, philosophy of science, law and morality, Aristotle, Kant, Marx, Bertrand Russell and other well-known philosophers.

Suggested High School Subjects
Advanced English, advanced social studies, mathematics including algebra, computer studies, foreign language.

General Interest Areas
Social sciences, mathematics, law, teaching, research.

Some Career Possibilities

philosopher	military officer	lawyer
clergy	diplomat	social worker
management consultant	education consultant	
college professor	freelance writer	

Some Related Majors

Bible studies	comparative literature	liberal arts
linguistics	sociology	political science
classics	foreign languages	
psychology	theological studies	

PHYSICAL CHEMISTRY

Description
Physical chemistry is the study of the properties and reactions of chemical substances in relation to the laws of physics. Once called "Theoretical Chemistry," it was originally concerned with the applications of the laws and insights of physics to simple chemical substances. Today, however, it is not so much a separate discipline as a type of approach to the study of the chemical and physical properties of both inorganic and organic substances.

Plan of Study
The plan of study follows the chemical model. At the lower-division level, extensive time is given to fundamental understanding of chemistry, biology, physics, and advanced mathematics (especially calculus). The upper-division level progresses to physical chemistry laboratory, physical inorganic chemistry, junior and senior seminars in current topics, and supervised independent research in physical chemistry. The student must be certain that the college program is accredited.

Expect to Take
Biology I and II, physics I and II, calculus I and II, chemistry I and II, introduction to physical chemistry, chemistry of macromolecules, photochemistry, junior/senior seminar in current topics, supervised research, internships.

Suggested High School Subjects
Advanced science including physics, advanced mathematics including calculus, computer studies, advanced science electives.

General Interest Areas
Science, mathematics, research, independent study and analysis.

Some Career Possibilities

analytical chemist	inorganic chemist	physician
college professor	laboratory technician	research scientist
consultant	organic chemist	teacher
engineer	physical chemist	technical writer

Some Related Majors

pharmacy	earth sciences	organic chem.
analytical chemistry	geochemistry	physics
biochemistry	inorganic chemistry	
chemical engineering	mathematics	

PHYSICAL EDUCATION

Description
This is the study of sport, athletics, exercise, and fitness. Historically, the major has prepared students to be teachers of physical education in schools. Now such programs have broadened the opportunities to include instruction in health and nutrition, aerobics and exercise science, as well as rehabilitation therapy or physical therapy. A provisional teaching certificate usually accompanies the degree in physical education; the range of possible career options that is currently available with this major bears careful research.

Plan of Study
The plan of study involves a core curriculum of academic courses, possibly including general chemistry or general physics, with physical education electives in the lower division. Upper-division work highlights skills in a number of sports, courses in teaching at the elementary or secondary school levels, coursework in nutrition, anatomy of movement, and techniques of coaching, a student teaching experience, and independent study of current issues in physical education.

Expect to Take
Individual sports, conditioning, activity leadership, anatomy and physiology, psychology of coaching, motor development and skill acquisition, student teaching, practicum.

Suggested High School Subjects
Science and mathematics, computer studies, extracurricular sports, social studies.

General Interest Areas
Sports, nutrition, teaching, coaching, social service.

Some Career Possibilities
athletic coach	camp director	drug counselor
physical therapist	psychologist	social worker
athletic trainer	college professor	elem. teacher
professional athlete	secondary school teacher	

Some Related Majors
dance	physical therapy	anatomy
health sciences	developmental	behavioral sci.
medical technology	psychology	biology
occupational therapy	pre-medicine	

PHYSICAL THERAPY

Description
This major is the study of the treatment of physical disabilities and disorders through the use of natural means (heat, radiation, electricity) and therapeutic techniques (exercise and massage). The therapist evaluates the problem and designs and implements a treatment plan. It is practiced in hospitals and other clinical settings, with the practitioner licensed by the state in which he or she wishes to work. Undergraduate programs accredited by the American Physical Therapy Association are recommended.

Plan of Study
The plan of study requires the completion of a very specific body of coursework during the first two years of college: chemistry, physics, advanced mathematics, comparative anatomy, psychology, and mammalian biology as the minimum. Admission to the upper division, where the student will specialize, will depend upon satisfactory completion of these courses and evaluation by a screening committee. A clinical internship of up to eighteen weeks of full-time practice will also be included in the accredited undergraduate program.

Expect to Take
Chemistry, physics, applied exercise physiology, therapy evaluation techniques, pathology, pharmacology, neuroscience, disease rehabilitation.

Suggested High School Subjects
Advanced science, advanced mathematics, computer studies, health, physical education, science electives.

General Interest Areas
Rehabilitation, science, physical education/fitness, patient care.

Some Career Possibilities
massage therapist	gerontologist	rehab therapist
occupational therapist	physician	research scientist
physical therapist	physician assistant	resort manager
chiropractor	physiologist	

Some Related Majors
anatomy	medical technology	pre-medicine
health sciences	nursing	
hospital/health care	occupational therapy	
administration	physical education	

PHYSICS, GENERAL

Description
Generally, physics is the study of the way the natural world works. Its approach is essentially experimental, axiomatic, and mathematical, seeking to understand a wide variety of phenomena as operating from a small number of basic principles. Physics encompasses knowledge of the fields of chemistry and biology, as well as a deep appreciation of mathematics. Physicists generally maintain that all science has physics as a common base and that the central thrust of research is to find some "unified theory" that explains the properties of matter in all its forms.

Plan of Study
Programs of study provide several alternatives. The B.S. in physics is the key to graduate study-leading to the Ph.D. or, in combination with a mathematics emphasis, toward an engineering/physics or a mathematics/physics dual major. Some colleges offer a B.A. in physics, combining coursework with secondary teaching certification. The plan of study requires courses in mechanics, quantum physics, atomic physics, kinetics, calculus, and computer science.

Expect to Take
Physics I--IV with lab, elementary and advanced mechanics, calculus I-III, thermal physics, electrodynamics, experimental physics, quantum theory.

Suggested High School Subjects
Advanced science including physics (AP preferred), advanced mathematics including calculus, computer studies.

General Interest Areas
Science, experimentation, research, mathematics.

Some Career Possibilities
physicist	laboratory technician	chemist
astrophysicist	biochemist	statistician
health physicist	biologist	
assayer	nuclear med technician	

Some Related Majors
applied mathematics	geophysics	physical chem.
engineering physics	biophysics	
astrophysics	mathematics engineering	

PHYSIOLOGICAL PSYCHOLOGY

Description
This major concerns the study of the functioning of the body's systems as a basis for behavior and mental processes. The methods of physiological psychology are largely experimental, involving use of techniques such as stimulation, electro-convulsive therapy, and hormonal and biochemical methods. Experimental psychology overlaps this field in several areas: sensory processes, motor functions, motivation, learning, and language development, to name a few.

Plan of Study
The plan of study is interdisciplinary at the lower-division level, with courses in psychology, mathematics, biological sciences, and humanities. At the upper-division level, the courses are divided between advanced biology topics and psychology specialties that highlight the connections between mental processes and organisms. Seminars, independent experimental research projects, and internships cap the program.

Expect to Take
Biology, chemistry, physics with lab, calculus through differential equations, anatomy and physiology, cognitive processes, social psychology, problems in physiological psychology, research projects.

Suggested High School Subjects
Advanced social studies, advanced science including biology and chemistry, mathematics including algebra and pre-calculus, computer studies.

General Interest Areas
Science, mathematics, experimentation, biology, medicine.

Some Career Possibilities
physiological psychologist	college professor	research scientist
clinical psychologist	experimental	lecturer
psychotherapist	psychologist	social psych.

Some Related Majors
anatomy	biology	dev. psych
experimental psychology	neuroscience	
behavioral sciences	clinical psychology	
human/animal physiology	psychology	

PLANT SCIENCES

Description Plant science is the study of economically important plant species, such as wheat, grain, oats, barley, and soybeans--their growth and reproduction, development and improvement, resistance to disease, environmental interactions, and other features. The undergraduate major usually terminates with a degree in agriculture, though specializations in agronomy, horticulture, plant breeding, and plant production are also available.

Plan of Study
The plan of study begins with coursework in the biological and physical sciences, including laboratory study, with selected electives in agriculture-related topics. At the upper-division level, advanced specialized coursework is supplemented with extensive field study to examine working agricultural systems. Specific crops also are studied; students interested in specific crops should examine programs carefully to find which schools offer which specializations.

Expect to Take
Biology with lab, chemistry with lab, physics with lab, calculus I and II, crop seeds, genetics, plant propagation, production skills, junior and senior seminars, field studies, supervised independent research.

Suggested High School Subjects
Advanced mathematics, advanced science, computer studies, science electives.

General Interest Areas
Farming, research, crop analysis, crop breeding.

Some Career Possibilities
plant scientist	agronomist	commodities
farm manager	laboratory assistant	geneticist
horticulturist	college professor	biochemist
biologist	parasitologist	technical writer

Some Related Majors
agricultural business/economics	landscape architecture	botany
entomology	bacteriology	
agronomy	soils/water management	

POLITICAL SCIENCE

Description
Broadly defined, this is the study of the organization of governments. It is also the study of the use of power to achieve goals, whether individual or national. As an undergraduate major, political science teaches students to differentiate among
the various kinds of political structures that presently exist, or have existed historically, to assess power struggles and conflicts within governments, and to explore relationships among nations. This major provides a good background for such careers as law, diplomacy, politics, international business, and related areas.

Plan of Study
The plan of study begins with a concentration on the humanities, especially social sciences such as psychology and sociology. At the upper-division level, emphasis is on the structure of governments, theories of politics, comparative political systems, utopian theories, and the like. Some colleges utilize an historical perspective in presenting this major; others stress cultural factors impacting upon political decisions or emphasize the "practical" approach to decision making.

Expect to Take
Introduction to psychology, social psychology, American government, European government and politics, political philosophy, international politics, public policy, decision making.

Suggested High School Subjects
English (especially reading and writing skills), advanced social studies, mathematics including algebra, science including biology and chemistry, computer literacy, foreign language.

General Interest Areas
Law, politics, government, public service, diplomacy, international government.

Some Career Possibilities

lawyer	political analyst	historian
international lawyer	embassy attaché	political scientist
corporate lawyer	political consultant	college professor
lecturer	freelance writer	
diplomat	political editor	

Some Related Majors

American studies	international relations	criminology
international business	area studies	urban studies
anthropology	secondary education	history

PRE-DENTISTRY

Description
Some dental health professionals must obtain a graduate degree in an area of specialization before being licensed to practice. A pre-dental undergraduate program is designed to prepare a student for entry into dental school. Approximately one to one-and-a-half years before admission to dental school, students must take the Dental Admission Test (DAT). Baccalaureate studies should be directed toward introducing the student to the knowledge expected on these exams.

Plan of Study
Strictly speaking, in most colleges, pre-dentistry is not a major program of study. Rather, it is an advisement program for pre-graduate study. After declaring a standard major, such as biology or chemistry, or even one that is not medically related, the student completes requirements for that major, along with the courses applicable toward graduate school admission. The student must examine and compare programs carefully to discover the one that is most suitable.

Expect to Take
Chemistry, biology with lab, physics with lab, advanced mathematics, human physiology, inorganic chemistry, foreign language.

Suggested High School Subjects
Advanced mathematics, advanced science, computer studies, selected science electives (especially related to biology), foreign language.

General Interest Areas
Medicine, science, dentistry, direct patient care.

Some Career Possibilities
anesthesiologist	microbiologist	pathologist
dentist	physician	veterinarian
dental surgeon	psychiatrist	physician
research scientist	urologist	

Some Related Majors
dental hygiene	anatomy	bioengineering
health sciences	anthropology	microbiology
pharmacy	biochemistry	

PRE-LAW

Description
This is rarely a true major area of study, but it enjoys such popularity among students along with pre-medicine and pre-dentistry—that it requires a page of explanation. Most colleges that offer this program explain that it is intended to be a guided program of liberal arts courses, taken with the close assistance of a pre-law adviser, a faculty member assigned to help students follow a plan of study that will likely lead to admission to a graduate school of law. Pre-law is a pre-professional endeavor and will not immediately lead to qualification to practice law.

Plan of Study
The plan of study includes a major field that will be recognized by a law school (from liberal arts to mathematics, accounting, or engineering), the maintenance of a competitive grade point average, and preparation for and completion of the Law School Admission Test (LSAT).

Expect to Take
English, social science, mathematics, science, foreign language, a declared major with appropriate coursework, electives possibly including a course that may be titled "pre-law for majors." This entire program must be closely advised and will vary from college to college. It may be advisable to major in an area which will provide a background for the student's future legal specialty, such as a business major for eventual study in corporate law.

Suggested High School Subjects
Advanced social studies, advanced English, foreign language, computer literacy.

General Interest Areas
Social sciences, law, business, diplomacy, foreign service, public service.

Some Career Possibilities

lawyer	civil lawyer	social worker
corporate lawyer	foreign service officer	teacher
military lawyer	civil servant	criminal lawyer
diplomat	clergy	

Some Related Majors

political science	English literature	philosophy
business administration	history	social sciences
criminology	international relations	urban studies

PRE-MEDICINE

Description
Pre-medicine is, as its name suggests, a program intended to prepare students to enter one of the health service fields, including physician. At the undergraduate level, it is usually an advisement program only. A health professions advisor or other similarly designated faculty member assists students in establishing the program of courses best suited for entry into an appropriate professional school, and aids students in preparing to take the Medical College Admission Test (MCAT). Most students planning to enter medical school actually major in biology, chemistry, or another life science, although such a major is not generally a firm requirement for admission.

Plan of Study
The plan of study is a very individualized one. The first emphasis is on a thorough grounding in the sciences; the core curriculum required for the B.S. or B.A. in the exact major is the next consideration; and electives in the humanities or foreign language are advised to round out the program. An important final component of the program is a pre-health professions committee evaluation as part of the student's application to medical school. There are some programs that combine the Baccalaureate degree with automatic admission to the college's medical school if certain requirements are met. Those programs are very selective.

Expect to Take
Biology I and II, general chemistry I and II, organic chemistry I and II, algebra and trigonometry I and II, general physics I and II.

Suggested High School Subjects
Advanced science and mathematics, computer studies, foreign language, science electives, advanced English and social studies

General Interest Areas
Science, medicine, health service professions.

Some Career Possibilities
physician	veterinarian	illustrator
osteopath	anesthesiologist	optometrist
podiatrist	biochemist	pharmacist
surgeon	chiropractor	

Some Related Majors
anatomy	biochemistry	health sciences
animal sciences	bioengineering	human/an. phys.
bacteriology	embryology	nuclear med. tech.

PSYCHOLOGY, GENERAL

Description
Psychology is the study of the physical and social origins of human thought and behavior, as well as the methods used to study them. While much of psychology is theoretical, it is mainly an empirically based science. Therefore, knowledge of methods for critically examining the various theories and experimental research is an essential skill.

Plan of Study
Psychology is a tree with many branches, including the following: clinical, social, experimental, developmental, abnormal, adolescent, and physiological psychology. The program of general psychology touches upon all of these, to prepare the student for graduate study in one area of choice. For a career, one may be required to go on to the Ph.D. in order to attain the qualifications needed for credentialed private practice in psychology, which may vary from State to State.

Expect to Take
General psychology, statistics, research methods, personality theory, learning theory, cognitive psychology, advanced mathematics, experimental methods, courses in specialized branches of psychology, independent research.

Suggested High School Subjects
Advanced social studies, mathematics including algebra, science (especially biology and chemistry), computer studies.

General Interest Areas
Science, experimentation, mathematics, social sciences.

Some Career Possibilities

psychologist	counselor	police officer
case worker	psychotherapist	social service aide
college professor	lawyer	probation officer
psychometrist	secondary school teacher	social worker

Some Related Majors

anthropology	physiological	dev. psych.
industrial psychology	psychology	social psychology
behavioral sciences	clinical social work	ed. psych.
philosophy	psychology for	sociology
clinical psychology	counseling	exp. psych.

PSYCHOLOGY FOR COUNSELING (COUNSELING PSYCHOLOGY)

Description
A branch of applied psychology, this major is the study of helping individuals to resolve personal, social, marital, career, or other conflicts. Personality theories, techniques of counseling and therapy, and administration of aptitude tests and interest inventories are among the chief concerns of this major. A small number of colleges offer this as an undergraduate major, but it is more often found as a graduate study.

Plan of Study
The undergraduate plan of study combines a comprehensive foundation in general psychological topics with upper-division work in theories of counseling, tests and measurements, and marital counseling, as well as practicum experiences and field externships with practicing counselors.

Expect to Take
General psychology, statistics and probability, algebra, adult human development, abnormal psychology, neuroses and psychoses, theories of counseling, counseling practicum, psychotherapy.

Suggested High School Subjects
Advanced social studies, mathematics including algebra, science including biology, computer literacy.

General Interest Areas
Helping people, social service, social science.

Some Career Possibilities
alcohol/drug counselor	psychotherapist	school counselor
probation officer	rehabilitation therapist	gerontologist
clergy	counseling psychologist	social worker

Some Related Majors
behavioral sciences	industrial psychology	dev. psych.
health sciences	clinical social work	psychology
clinical psychology	personnel management	ed. psych.

PUBLIC HEALTH

Description
This major is concerned with protecting and improving the health of the community rather than that of the individual. Municipal, county, and state health departments employ public health workers to inspect food-related industries to ensure healthful produce, meat, milk, and other consumables. On a broader level, the federal government maintains the Public Health Service which works within the Department of Agriculture, Labor Department, and the Food and Drug Administration. Other titles for this major include public health laboratory science, public health nursing, and community health.

Plan of Study
The plan of study at the undergraduate level requires close advisement by a faculty member. Coursework in the biological sciences and chemistry, with electives in advanced mathematics, fills the lower-division schedule. Later, courses in health care administration are supplemented by advanced health-care related science courses such as epidemiology and biostatistics. Finally, advanced seminars in independent research projects and internships complete the program.

Expect to Take
Organic chemistry, toxicology, vector control, medical sociology, human services management, ethical issues in health policy, health law, seminars, statistics, research projects.

Suggested High School Subjects
Advanced social studies, science and mathematics, at least one foreign language, computer studies, science electives.

General Interest Areas
Science, health, community service, mathematics.

Some Career Possibilities
public health educator	college professor	lawyer
food/drug inspector	customs inspector	health official
public health officer	community organization	social worker
alcohol counselor	director	

Some Related Majors
bacteriology	hospital/health care	pharmacy
biochemistry	administration	physical therapy
environmental science	medical technology	
health sciences	nursing	

RADIO AND TELEVISION

Description
This communications specialty involves the organization, creation, and production of programs through the electronic media. This is generally a hands-on major in which the student is exposed to the theoretical aspects of radio/television work and then becomes directly involved in actual production. Colleges offering this program as a true major should be equipped with state-of-the-art technology to conduct instruction. A college visit to view the facilities is highly recommended. Participation in campus radio or television station operations is often required, either as an on-air performer, or a studio technician, or both. Internships with nearby radio or television stations may be available.

Plan of Study
The plan of study incorporates liberal arts courses at the outset. During the junior year, time is often spent in a laboratory environment, learning about the techniques for operating a radio or television station and producing short pieces or documentaries.

Expect to Take
The communications industry, electronic media programming, communications regulation and policy, television documentary, social aspects of electronic media, techniques of radio/television production, public speaking.

Suggested High School Subjects
Advanced English, English electives, speech and/or broadcasting electives, social studies, computer studies.

General Interest Areas
Communications, social sciences, arts, electronics.

Some Career Possibilities
radio/TV producer	news editor	station owner
copywriter	station manager	station director
management consultant	radio/TV broadcaster	technical writer

Some Related Majors
advertising	journalism	dramatic arts
fine arts	communications	
cinematography	media study	

REAL ESTATE

Description
Real estate is the study of the purchase and sale of land, property, and buildings—both commercial and residential; and the analysis of the legal and economic problems involved in such transactions. The bachelor's degree is often combined with the study of urban development. The four-year program develops an understanding of the formulation and application of political and economic regulations and policies impacting the real estate industry. Certificate and two-year associate's degree programs are also available to prepare for employment in the field.

Plan of Study
The plan of study begins with a business administration core of courses. At the upper-division level, specialized courses are offered in topics such as financial decision-making methods, data analysis in real estate valuation and appraisal, management of residential and commercial property, the operation of markets, and legal principles in real estate dealings. Internships with housing agencies, large real estate corporations, and banks also may be available.

Expect to Take
Housing economics, real estate policies, urban development, investment strategy, residential development, real estate transactions.

Suggested High School Subjects
English composition, advanced mathematics, science, computer studies, electives in business and social studies.

General Interest Areas
Business, mathematics, entrepreneurship.

Some Career Possibilities

real estate sales	estate planner	specialist lawyer
bank loan officer	analyst	market researcher
realtor/broker	international business	teacher
business manager	accountant	urban planner

Some Related Majors

accounting	business economics	international bus.
banking/finance	economics	marketing
business administration	insurance	mathematics

SECONDARY EDUCATION

Description
The program in secondary education leads to a career in teaching in grades seven through twelve. Subject-matter competency is the first requirement, and students must be accepted into an academic department such as English, mathematics, science, or foreign language in addition to applying to the education department for enrollment in the certification program. Acceptance is not usually automatic; a minimum grade point average is usually required, as well as a personal interview in the education department, and, depending upon local regulations, the passing of some qualifying tests.

Plan of Study
The plan of study begins with general education courses in the arts and sciences. Students also undertake work in the academic concentration during this time, as well as elective coursework. At the upper-division level, continued academic study is supplemented with courses in secondary education foundations, methods, and other courses needed for certification. A student-teaching component is required. Depending upon the academic major being pursued, a B.A. or B.S. degree is awarded.

Expect to Take
Foundations of secondary education, method courses in academic subjects, educational psychology, adolescent development, classroom management, introduction to learning disabilities, student teaching, independent study, internship.

Suggested High School Subjects
Advanced English and social studies, advanced mathematics and science, foreign language, computer studies.

General Interest Areas
Education, working with children, social work fields, subject-matter interest.

Some Career Possibilities
secondary school teacher	school counselor	social worker
adult education teacher	college professor	program director
school administrator	educational consultant	
clergy	lawyer	

Some Related Majors
business administration	insurance	personnel
philosophy	pre-law	elementary ed.
foreign languages	liberal arts	
political science	psychology	

SOCIAL PSYCHOLOGY

Description
This major is the study of the thoughts, feelings, and behaviors exhibited or experienced by individuals in group settings. Social psychologists are interested in such topics as the basis for racial segregation and prejudice, how television violence influences individual aggression, and the effects of childhood experiences on adult personality.

Plan of Study
The plan of study requires a broad acquaintance with general psychology and related topics, such as statistics and measurements, at the lower-division level. Later coursework concentrates on social, behavioral, and experimental topics such as personality theory and abnormal psychology. Field work, specialty seminars, and an internship experience complete the study.

Expect to Take
General psychology, science with laboratory, college algebra, statistics I and II, analysis of psychological data, human learning, tests and measurements, practicum in social development, computer applications in psychology.

Suggested High School Subjects
Advanced social studies, mathematics including algebra, science including biology, computer studies.

General Interest Areas
Human development, research, science.

Some Career Possibilities
consultant	psychotherapist	social psychologist
psychometrist	counselor	lecturer
college professor	social caseworker	technical writer
counseling psychologist	editor/writer	management

Some Related Majors
industrial psychology	clinical psychology	psych for couns.
behavioral sciences	psychology	exp. psych.
personnel management	clinical social work	social sciences

SOCIAL SCIENCES, GENERAL

Description
The general major in the social sciences is a survey of the many fields within the discipline. The purpose of the major is to understand more clearly the attributes and difficulties of human beings in cultural, intercultural, personal, and interpersonal contexts. Students examine the psycho-social forces operating in contemporary life and evaluate these forces historically.

Plan of Study
The plan of study includes introductory courses in a variety of social science fields, such as economics, history, political science, sociology, and psychology. In addition, methodology and research tools are taught for use in scholarly analysis of local, national, and international topics of current concern. With special advisement, this major also may offer concentrations for the pre-law student. Some schools coordinate this major with teacher education, leading to certification in social studies.

Expect to Take
Introductory and advanced history, sociology, economics, anthropology, psychology, government, statistics, research methodology, independent study or supervised research in current topics.

Suggested High School Subjects
English (especially reading and writing skills), advanced social studies, mathematics including algebra, science including biology, computer literacy, foreign language.

General Interest Areas
Liberal arts, human services, law, politics.

Some Career Possibilities
anthropologist	editor/writer	consultant
college professor	education consultant	secondary teacher
counselor	government civil servant	social scientist
clergy	lawyer	social worker

Some Related Majors
American studies	political science	sociology
anthropology	psychology	elementary ed.
clinical social work	secondary education	
history	social psychology	

SOCIOLOGY

Description
Sociology is the scientific study of human society, its development and institutions, and the interactions of individuals between each other and with those institutions. As societal changes have accelerated in recent decades, the discipline has grown rapidly. The field employs its own techniques to assess the changes and to prescribe ways for individuals and institutions to cope.

Plan of Study
The plan of study includes a basic foundation in the humanities and coursework in such areas as demography, urban, suburban, and rural communities, mass media, family life, and legal structures. Sociological techniques such as survey research, field observation, and experimentation are stressed. Field research on topics of current interest are required; internship opportunities may be available.

Expect to Take
Introduction to psychology, social structure, statistics and probability, urban living, demographics, computer modeling of social environments, coping with social change, democratic versus totalitarian societies, primitive societies, field research, internships.

Suggested High School Subjects
Social studies, mathematics including algebra, computer literacy, foreign language, social science electives if possible, such as psychology and anthropology.

General Interest Areas
Law, history, political science, research, data collection and analysis.

Some Career Possibilities
probation officer	psychologist	social scientist
freelance writer	government researcher	lecturer
college professor	research scientist	social worker
management consultant	lawyer	sociologist

Some Related Majors
American studies	secondary education	clinical soc. work
psychology	behavioral sciences	urban studies
anthropology	social psychology	criminology

SOFTWARE ENGINEERING

Description
Software engineering is the study of the design, development, testing, and production of software for computer and other device applications, using the principles of engineering as a base. The major combines the essentials of electrical and mechanical engineering, together with fundamentals of computer science, to create software products for use in business, education, science, industry, and entertainment.

Plan of Study
The first two years of the program are heavily laden with typical engineering basics: calculus each semester, physics, computer programming, fundamentals of engineering, and so on. The upper division continues with selected engineering courses, focusing on software development skills, and usually concludes with the completion of a supervised project. Internship and cooperative work experiences are highly important at this level, to see up-close the challenges of this rapidly evolving specialty. The curriculum of the related major in Computer Engineering, which focuses more on hardware, should also be examined closely for those interested in the field.

Expect to Take
Calculus I-IV, chemistry with lab, physics with lab, computer programming, probability and statistics, software development I and II, software project, internship or co-op experience.

Suggested High School Subjects
Advanced math, advanced science, computer science, computer art graphics elective.

General Interest Areas
Science, computers, creativity, software, app development.

Some Career Possibilities
computer programmer	computer hardware	systems analyst
app developer	developer	technical writer
inventor	entrepreneur	customer support
college professor	software developer	
computer animator	software technician	

Some Related Majors
computer engineering	business statistics	op. research
computer science	electrical engineering	systems analysis
applied mathematics	mathematics	telecomm.

SOILS AND WATER MANAGEMENT

Description
This major is the study of the uses of soil, water, air, and other natural resources to promote plant and animal growth. It is an important study in the production of food and the management of natural and urban environments. Found primarily in colleges within a department of agriculture, this major trains students to be managers, using the principles of physical science and engineering and applying them to practical needs.

Plan of Study
The lower-division plan of study includes the fundamentals of chemistry and physics, advanced mathematics and engineering, and electives in botany and biology. The upper division plan of study includes courses in earth and soil sciences. Students seeking certification as soil scientists by the Soil Science Society of America will be required to take additional courses in botany, plant pathology, and silviculture. Students also are encouraged to take courses in computer science, related mathematics, and statistical research.

Expect to Take
Agricultural mechanics, soils laboratory, farm structures, agricultural engineering, soil fertility, principles of agriculture, water control, pollution technology, field studies, advanced seminars, independent research.

Suggested High School Subjects
Advanced mathematics through calculus, advanced science through physics, computer studies, selected college-preparatory business electives such as business law or management.

General Interest Areas
Agriculture, earth sciences, mathematics, environmental science, research.

Some Career Possibilities

park ranger	water purity chemist	geophysicist
research scientist	chemical engineer	hydrologist
soil scientist	ecologist	lab. technician
treatment plant manager	environmentalist	oceanographer

Some Related Majors

agronomy	ecology	marine biology
biology	environmental	microbiology
chemical engineering	engineering	oceanography
earth sciences	environmental science	

SPECIAL EDUCATION

Description
This is the study of the education of handicapped persons. "Special Education" is an umbrella term that includes education of emotionally disturbed, learning disabled, physically handicapped, intellectually disabled, and multiple handicapped individuals. Most programs seek to qualify the student to teach in public schools, either elementary or secondary, as well as in private, residential settings and state institutions. Interested students should examine undergraduate programs carefully, as they vary widely in quality, type of degree awarded, and qualifications for teacher certification in the state where one plans to teach.

Plan of Study
The plan of study emphasizes a core curriculum in arts and sciences at the lower-division level, with elective courses in education, as part of the certification requirement. Upper division study focuses on study of the various types of learning disabilities and handicapping conditions, their causes, diagnosis, treatment, and remediation. Enabling the handicapped individual to manage his or her life and returning that person to the least restrictive environment are the goals. Independent study, research, and a student teaching experience completes the program.

Expect to Take
Developmental psychology, behavior disorders, education of the severely handicapped, statistics, classroom management, learning characteristics of the intellectually handicapped.

Suggested High School Subjects
Advanced social studies, advanced science and mathematics, computer studies, social science electives if offered.

General Interest Areas
Social science, social work, education, handicapped persons.

Some Career Possibilities
secondary school teacher	counselor	clinical psych.
elementary school teacher	anthropologist	college instructor
school administrator	psychiatrist	school psych.
rehabilitation therapist	clergy	social worker

Some Related Majors
secondary education	behavioral sciences	pre-medicine
elementary education	physical therapy	dev. psychology
occupational therapy	clinical psychology	social psych.

SPEECH PATHOLOGY AND AUDIOLOGY

Description
This major is the study of the evaluation, diagnosis, prevention, and treatment of speech and hearing disorders. Usually found within the health sciences department, the major is intended for students preparing for work in schools and medical and paramedical facilities. Students electing this major usually must demonstrate proficiency in reading, writing, and oral communications and usually be free of voice, hearing, and speaking problems.

Plan of Study
The plan of study is largely scientific in nature with emphasis on physiology and anatomy as well as the study of therapeutic modes for specific pathologies. Lower-division preparation includes a core curriculum of courses which may be evaluated by a screening committee of faculty before admission to the upper division is granted. Because this is a direct patient-care health service, extensive experience through practicum or internship in a health care facility is most likely required during the senior year.

Expect to Take
Speech and language development, phonetics, anatomy and physiology, anatomy of auditory and vocal mechanisms, clinical practicum, counseling in auditory and speech pathology.

Suggested High School Subjects
Advanced science including biology and physics, advanced mathematics, computer literacy, related science electives.

General Interest Areas
Science, patient care, hearing and speech therapy.

Some Career Possibilities
audiologist	speech teacher	lab. technician
speech pathologist	psychologist	
hearing/speech therapist	college professor	

Some Related Majors
communications	education of the deaf	industrial psych.
linguistics	neuroscience	special education
dramatic arts	educational psychology	
music	nursing	

SYSTEMS ANALYSIS

Description
Systems analysis is the study of the organizational structure and behavior of multiple sets of elements. Most frequently, the term is used to denote the study of computer languages and their possible interactions and applications. The major is a specialty within the broad area of mathematics and usually requires above-average conceptual skills and a strong background in advanced mathematics.

Plan of Study
The plan of study includes courses in advanced mathematics with selected electives in computer programming, computer languages, and advanced statistical methods. Few colleges offer a pure major in systems analysis at the undergraduate level. More often it is an option within a computer science or computer engineering program. Some colleges use terms such as "Systems Planning," or "Computer Systems" to describe their offerings. Others offer dual major programs in systems analysis/engineering or systems analysis/business administration. The field of available choices should be searched carefully.

Expect to Take
Physics I and II, calculus I-III, data structures, statistics I and II, operating systems, program language laboratory I and II, analysis of program language, independent research.

Suggested High School Subjects
Advanced mathematics including calculus, advanced science including physics, computer studies, mathematics electives including statistics and probability.

General Interest Areas
Mathematics, computers, analysis, research.

Some Career Possibilities
systems analyst	college professor	demographer
systems engineer	comptroller	entrepreneur
government analyst	computer engineer	
statistician	computer programmer	

Some Related Majors
accounting	business administration	computer science
applied mathematics	business economics	international bus.
banking/finance	business statistics	mathematics

TELECOMMUNICATIONS

Description
Telecommunications is the study of the technology used to send and receive information over a distance. While the field has many applications, this major explores familiar as well as emerging technologies, such as fiber optics and satellite communications. Computer hardware and software, cellular telephone systems, applications, and Government regulations are also important. The thrust of telecommunications technology is to find new and creative ways to improve the speed and quality of communications.

Plan of Study
Schools offering a true telecommunications major will have one or both of two options: technical concentration or management concentration. The technical study emphasizes coursework in selected electrical engineering and technical electronics topics, with a view toward understanding how to create new applications of communications technology. The management option prepares students for supervisory and leadership positions in telecommunications organizations, as well as an understanding of telecommunications regulatory policies and security. Many programs will include a mandatory externship or cooperative work experience as part of the degree requirement. This is a growing major; programs will, therefore, vary widely in quality. College offerings must be examined carefully for content and accreditation. College admissions offices should be consulted directly to ask key questions about program strength to understand if their program leads to your goal.

Expect to Take
Advanced mathematics, physics I and II, telecommunications concepts, network engineering, communications law, electronic devices, internship/work experience.

Suggested High School Subjects
Advanced math, advanced science, computer science, computer programming, technology.

General Interest Areas
Science, mathematics, computers, research.

Some Career Possibilities
communications engineer	electronics buyer/sales	network security
electronics engineer	software engineer	
electrical engineer	quality control engineer	

Some Related Majors
applied mathematics	computer science	systems analysis
engineering	physics	
mechanical engineering	electrical engineering	

THEOLOGICAL STUDIES

Description
Theology is the study of God and the relationship of God to people. In this major, the existence of God, belief in God, and forms of worship are examined. This highly specialized major is ordinarily pursued by students whose goal is to enter the clergy, but others may use this major for a more academic purpose. It may lead to the more frequently found graduate major or professional level study.

Plan of Study
The plan of study includes a core humanities curriculum, electives in one or two classical languages such as Greek or Latin (for the reading of selected texts in the original versions), courses in ontology (the study of being), epistemology (the study of knowing), ethics, world religions, sacred texts, writings of theologians past and present, and the evolution of theological thought, and independent research projects and seminars. Field experiences such as teaching assignments and missionary externships also may be required.

Expect to Take
Psychology, sociology, beginning/intermediate Latin/Greek, God in history, pastoral counseling, comparative theology, Bible study, textual exegesis, advanced seminars, independent research.

Suggested High School Subjects
Advanced social studies, computer studies, foreign languages, speech.

General Interest Areas.
Religion, social work, volunteer/missionary activity, ancient history.

Some Career Possibilities
clergy	school administrator	counselor
theological writer	college instructor	psychiatrist
missionary	therapist	psychologist
teacher	social worker	

Some Related Majors
anthropology	Bible studies	secondary ed.
foreign languages	psychology for couns.	communications
behavioral sciences	sociology	
philosophy	classics	

TOXICOLOGY

Description
Toxicology is called the science of poisons. This study investigates the physical and chemical properties of poisons and their biological effects as well as their detection and treatment. This requires understanding toxicity levels, degrees of hazard, and dosages needed to reverse damage.

Plan of Study
Several specialties exist within the major: forensic toxicology (medical and legal aspects of poisons), industrial toxicology (analyzing pollutants within the air of water), economic toxicology (understanding of chemicals used in drugs, food additives, pesticides, and cosmetics), and environmental toxicology (studying the cumulative effects of chemicals on the environment).

Expect to Take
Principles of toxicology, immunology, microbiology, antibodies, antigen complexes, microbial toxicology, cell biology, supervised research, field studies in toxicology.

Suggested High School Subjects
Advanced science including physics, advanced mathematics including calculus, computer studies, science electives.

General Interest Areas
Research, environmental concerns, statistics, poisons and antidotes.

Some Career Possibilities

toxicologist	parasitologist	environmentalist
biochemist	consultant	technical writer
microbiologist	pathologist	
college professor	corporate researcher	

Some Related Majors

bacteriology	biology	histology
embryology	marine biology	chemistry
biochemistry	cytology	zoology

TRANSPORTATION

Description
The transportation major is the study of the movement of people or property by land, sea, or air. Besides being concerned with scheduling costs, rate charges, warehousing, safety limits, and the changes being brought about by advancing technology, this major also studies the environmental and ecological impact of building roads, railways, and airports. A program with the Department of Business Administration, this major prepares students for employment in the private sector and with public agencies in the areas of transportation policy and administration.

Plan of Study
The plan of study begins with a core of business courses, including work in accounting and possible electives in finance. The upper-division curriculum moves through advanced specialized courses and concludes with senior year seminars, a possible independent research project, and internships.

Expect to Take
Principles of transportation, accounting, organizational behavior, warehousing, cost analysis, business law, transportation regulations, seminars, independent projects.

Suggested High School Subjects
Social studies electives including economics, mathematics including algebra, computer studies, college-preparatory business electives including business law and introduction to business.

General Interest Areas
Business, economics, management, travel

Some Career Possibilities
traffic manager	industrial manager	urban planner
transportation engineer	policy analyst	wholesaler
accountant	route scheduler	analyst
contract administrator	transportation manager	

Some Related Majors
accounting	business economics	mathematics
banking/finance	communications	urban studies
business administration	economics marketing	naval arch.

URBAN STUDIES

Description
In general, this major is the study of how cities work. The program examines the organization and administration of cities and the delivery of services such as education, health, police, sanitation, and housing; and analyzes the process of public, urban policy-making. The effect of government and politics on this process is also a subject of concern.

Plan of Study
The plan of study is generally viewed as interdisciplinary. Coursework is geared toward developing the skills and concepts needed for analysis of urban problems within the context of such areas as sociology, history, economics, anthropology, and politics. Field experiences and internships with urban agencies of government are encouraged (required in some colleges), and allow students to see the working of groups in formulating policy and responding to the needs of citizens.

Expect to Take
Urban anthropology, the rise of the city, politics in the urban scene, history of the American city, social science research methods, social psychology, urban contemporary issues, field study, independent research.

Suggested High School Subjects
English, advanced reading and writing skills, advanced social sciences, foreign language, psychology, sociology, computer studies, electives.

General Interest Areas
History, anthropology, politics, sociology, research.

Some Career Possibilities
urban affairs specialist	publications editor	sociologist
political analyst	entrepreneur	gov. worker
college professor	social scientist	lawyer
consultant	freelance writer	

Some Related Majors
real estate	environmental	public health
American studies	engineering	social psych.
business administration	journalism	sociology
economics	political science	

ZOOLOGY

Description
Zoology is the study of animals. It is the in-depth investigation of the physiology, behavior, characteristics, development, and evolution of animals. Classification (taxonomy), genetics, and embryology are areas of interest. It may be pursued individually as a major area, or combined with biology, chemistry, physics, or another life science in a dual-major program. Zoology also may be used as pre-professional preparation for a veterinary medicine program.

Plan of Study
The plan of study is designed to immerse the student in life sciences. Specialized topics in animal physiology are emphasized, including ornithology, herpetology, and ichthyology to name a few. The program is intentionally rigorous.

Expect to Take
Invertebrate zoology, biology, vertebrate physiology, comparative anatomy, organic chemistry, physics with lab, microbiology, virology.

Suggested High School Subjects
Advanced science, including biology (AP preferred) and chemistry, computer studies.

General Interest Areas
Science, medicine, mathematics, research, experimentation.

Some Career Possibilities
zoologist	laboratory technician	college prof.
marine biologist	biochemist	pest controller
veterinarian	biologist	ecologist
anatomist	paleontologist	entomologist

Some Related Majors
agricultural bus./eco.	human/animal phys.	biology
genetics	bacteriology	microbiology
animal sciences	marine biology	entomology